GOING PLACES AND DOING THINGS:

THE MODERN WOMAN'S GUIDE TO LIVING WILD AND FREE

Kristine Hudson

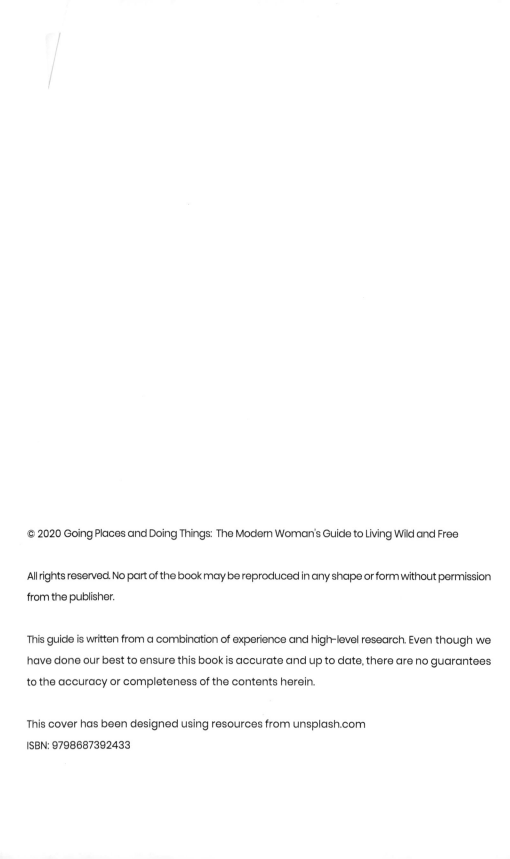

ISBN: 9798687392433

Reviews

Reviews and feedback help improve this book and the author. If you enjoy this book, we would greatly appreciate it if you could take a few moments to share your opinion and post a review on Amazon.

Contents

HOW TO CHOOSE THE ULTIMATE SIDE-HUSTLE

HOW TO LIVE THE DREAM:

THINGS EVERY VAN LIFER NEEDS TO KNOW

Kristine Hudson

Section 1: Making the Big Decision

There's a certain romance to the idea of living on the road. Traveling wherever the wind blows. Leaving nothing except footprints. Taking nothing but pictures.

The media is awash with images of attractive, wind-swept people, staring out of their windows at an awe-inspiring vista. Mountains, oceans, and fields so far and wide, you can hardly see the horizon. All these images make van living look like an incredible option. Not only do you get to shed the boring, stale, workaday lifestyle, but you get to wake up wherever you want.

To many, van living is the ultimate goal. It is the dream that just won't go away. While there's tons of material in the media explaining how amazing van life is, there is little to help you prepare for the reality of life on the road.

We'll explore what it takes to hack a nomadic lifestyle in the 21st century, with road tips provided from actual American van dwellers. Throughout this book, you'll find "Advice from the Road," which contains tips, tricks, and details provided by folks who have personally practiced the van lifestyle.

We'll start with all the considerations you'll need to keep in mind before making the decision to follow your wanderlust. We'll also go through the process of choosing your new home, as well as things to consider when creating and utilizing space. Budgeting, as well as managing income and expenditures, is also a huge part of van life. We'll help you get packed and ready to hit the trails, with some tips and tricks for staying happy and learning to find your home on the road.

You might be surprised at how involved the process is, but bear in mind that this is always your adventure. You can ramp up or tame the journey to meet your preferred lifestyle. After all, this is *your* life's dream!

Chapter 1: Why Do I Want to Live in a Van?

Before you start the engine and bid farewell to your friends and family — before you even have an engine to start — you must get in touch with your dream. This may sound a bit New Age, but the reality is that you are about to commit to a very significant lifestyle change by living in a van. Whether you have a regular nine-to-five job that you're sick of, or have been a freewheeling freelancer for years, van living is nothing like what you have experienced to date.

You will not be able to come home. If you have a rough day, you won't be able to "just stay in and order a pizza." The routines that have come to rule your life will no longer exist.

If hearing that makes your heart beat a little faster, you're not alone. The primary reason people choose van life is because they are sick of having a home and a yard, or an apartment and neighbors. They're tired of commuting to work. They don't want to spend an entire weekend cleaning floors and dusting knick-knacks. They want to live.

If you identify with this, you're on the right track. But here's one important question to ask yourself: By living on the road, what do you hope to achieve? What deep, burning need in your life will van living satisfy, and are you prepared to make a significant number of sacrifices to find that lifestyle?

Let us point out before you start feeling less certain about van living: there are different types of van living experiences.

First, there's the type of Van Lifers who maintain their home and daily lifestyle but use their van as a mobile escape. In previous decades, truly adventurous families had vacation properties, such as beach condos or lakeside cabins. The modern twist on this is to make the holiday home a van, so adventure may take place anywhere you can imagine to drive.

Then there are the semi-permanent nomads. These folks may have a PO Box in a permanent location. They may live full time in the van, but they stay tied to a particular area, whether that be an RV park, long-term campground, or the general vicinity. They may take off for an adventure now and again, but they migrate only around a certain radius.

Lastly, there are the true devotees. These folks plan to see as much as possible and do as much as they can before their time on this planet expires. They hope to never see the same sunset or sunrise — though if they do, they maintain it's purely because they wanted to see that view one more time. These folks don't plan to land on terra firma any time soon and are fully prepared to have all their needs fulfilled by life on the road.

You may fit firmly within one of these categories. You might find yourself somewhere in shades in between. Remember, there is no "wrong way" to organize your dreams. The goal of van life is to fulfill a need you have deep in your soul, and if your soul decides it wants to come home and do a load of laundry, that does not mean you're not accomplishing your dream.

When it comes to van living, there are a few aspects of the lifestyle that tend to be magnets to most people considering the option. Let's explore those in more detail.

The Chance to Live Off-Grid
While "keeping up with the Joneses'" has been part of the American Dream for over a century, there are many who are no longer impressed with this ideal. A larger house might be a great fantasy, but that involves a heftier house payment — which means working more hours. And a bigger house means more "stuff," like furniture and decorations. Owning more means increased upkeep, higher utility bills, taking care of a bigger lawn, etc. For some folks, this sounds less like the American Dream and more like a terrifying nightmare.

A van does not have a mortgage, though you might find yourself making payments on your roaming home — we'll discuss that more later. A van doesn't have utility bills. A van doesn't have an attic to maintain or a basement that floods when it rains. A van doesn't have noisy neighbors. You will do no yard work.

But that doesn't mean it's completely carefree. A van is a mechanical invention, and it can break down. Windows can crack. Tires can blow. You'll need to find new ways of creating power. You will not have running water unless you create that option. If anything breaks, you will have to take care of it, and immediately. While van living does mean you'll be living off the grid, it does not mean you'll live without responsibility.

The Ability to Be Self-Sustaining

Urban and suburban lifestyles require constant connection. You have neighbors. You have coworkers. You have friends. Your social obligations require you to continually connect with these individuals in order to sustain your network and relationships. How much time do you have to yourself?

Traveling the country solo, with just the wind as your copilot may seem like the best way to completely disconnect and shed all these social responsibilities. You have the chance to be alone with your own mind and learn who you are. You can discover how your mind and soul work, and uncover the mystery of who you want to become before your time on this planet draws to a close.

When you work 40-80 hours a week, 52 weeks of the year, you lose the connection with yourself and become the routine that maintains your lifestyle. Being on the road will tear you away from what you've known as life, and guide you to understanding who you really are.

And that means completely upending that routine. What will you do on Saturday mornings, if not going to meet friends for brunch, followed by cleaning the bathroom? When Monday morning arrives, how will you greet the day if you don't have to shower and get ready for work before the sun rises?

For many of us, our lifestyle is determined by what we need to do to keep doing the same thing. When you live on the road, you no longer have to sustain these patterns. While you certainly can continue to work in an office if that's your preference, you won't feel the pressure to work 12-hour days to pay the bills. It certainly won't take you multiple hours to clean the bathroom. Every aspect of your life will be simplified to the most basic needs, rather than creating a level of comfort.

Will you be able to live without guidelines, restrictions, or limitations of someone else? Will you choose instead to learn how to self-sustain, the way humans were intended to live?

The Freedom to Roam

When you no longer live under the demands of someone else's schedule, you have the ability to create your own agenda. This means you can go anywhere you want. You can see what you want to see. Do what you want to do. You don't have to be in the boardroom for a meeting at 3 pm every day. You don't have to take a day off work to wait for the repair technician because the cable isn't working. You have the freedom to dictate your own schedule, and your home has four rubber wheels that are designed to take you anywhere.

This may sound absolutely ideal for many, but it can also cause a bit of anxiety for others. Choice paralysis is real, and some people might have a hard time deciding what to do next. After all, hunting and gathering is no longer a truly viable option in the United States, so following the herds and water sources is not a requirement for survival.

The freedom to roam also means you have to decide where you're going to go. You may be the type of person who has to know where you're going to be on any given day, and that's a hard habit to break. When it is midnight and you're driving through a severe thunderstorm, you might regret not having found a place to park and turn in for the night. After all, though you may shed the responsibilities of suburban life, you'll never get past biological needs!

Even at its most liberating, van life still demands a certain amount of planning and research. While you'll have the ability to go anywhere you want, you still have to acknowledge the practicalities, legalities, and realities that await you.

See the World on Your Own Time

Now that you are no longer living under someone else's agenda, you have to create your own. This doesn't have to be a hard-set "to-do" list of daily chores, but instead, a list of goals and accomplishments you'd like to have under your belt in time.

Before you hit the road, create a list of places you'd like to see, or things you'd like to do. Want to summit El Capitan? Fantastic. Have a burning desire to see the sun rise on the southernmost point of the country? Excellent. Consider themes and key points of interest that really get your blood pumping. Now that you have this freedom, it's time to make the most of it.

Once you are on the road, you truly have the ability to see the world. If you choose to make van living a full-time lifestyle, then this is not a vacation. You do not have to be back in the office in three days' time. You don't need to hire someone to water the plants. If you are going to be a part-time road warrior, however, then you will need to adjust accordingly, which makes having an agenda even more important. After all, the reason you've chosen to live in a van, instead of a tiny house or exotic cave, is because you embrace mobility.

Consider the Alternative

Now that you've really defined why you feel compelled to live in a van, consider the option of not living in a van.

That's right — the time has come to ask yourself why this is so important. One way to make your desires truly transparent is to look at the situation from the flip side.

What if you don't pursue this? What if you just stay home, continue working your job, making sure your knick-knacks don't get dusty? Maybe you go camping every weekend to scratch that wanderlust itch, but you don't go all the way into van living. Would this be something that you would regret?

Living in a van is demanding. Physically, you'll find you have to spend a significant amount of time driving. Your gym routine is likely a thing of the past, too, and you'll have to find ways to feed yourself that don't involve a full-sized kitchen. Emotionally, you will be alone with your thoughts, all day, every day. Are you prepared to keep yourself entertained? Are you comfortable addressing all of the thoughts, hopes, dreams, and emotions that have been ignored while you go with the urban flow? Mentally, you're going to have to prepare for a new set of dangers and challenges. While remaining open to rewards that would never be possible when living in a two bedroom walk-up.

Successful van life is more than just knowing how to set up your bathroom and innovative storage. It is far more than dangling tan legs out the window or watching the sun rise and set in new, amazing places. This is an opportunity to shed not only your electric bill, but every expectation that has ever been made of you and your abilities. You will need to learn a new set of survival skills, and the things that made you feel "comfortable" in a home-dwelling lifestyle will no longer be the same.

In many ways, van living is an entirely new life, and this is a journey that will require dedication and preparation in order to serve you well. You will learn much along the way; in fact, many would argue that you'll learn far more about life when living on the road. However, you have to be prepared to execute those skills and to be ready for a new set of challenges.

Chapter 2: The Reality of Van Living - Doing Your Homework

Before making the decision to commit to van life, it is important that you understand all the challenges and potential hazards that come with the lifestyle. While you have a new and exciting level of freedom, you are going to encounter a new level of responsibility. Not only do you have complete control over where you roam, but you are required to solve every problem that might arise.

This is not to say these problems are too hard to solve. In fact, being prepared before you hit the road will help turn these problems into a variety of inconveniences, rather than taking all the zest out of van living. You will find that one of the key elements to a successful van lifestyle is planning and preparation, which can begin as soon as you start day-dreaming about the possibilities.

Let's look at some of the key areas in which you'll need to practice good planning and preparation. This includes: knowing how to keep up with van maintenance, being aware of your equipment, keeping it in good working order, and finding places to park and catch up on rest.

Van Maintenance

Taking care of yourself will be critical on the road, but taking care of your van will be equally important. Therefore, you will need to learn some basic van maintenance.

There are many aspects of vehicle repair and preservation that are relatively simple and can be conducted on nearly any flat service. Being able to check, monitor, and replenish your fluids is a great place to start. Oil, coolant, transmission fluid, brake fluid, and power steering fluid are all things that will need constant observation when you live on the road. They need very little automotive skill to learn where to find the input point, what type to buy, and when to top off your supply.

You may want to invest a little more effort into your overall maintenance skills in order to preserve your overall autonomy. There are two basic facts that apply to any van living situation:
1.   A vehicle in motion will require more maintenance, more frequently.
2.   Vans require specialized mechanics in many cases. Some vans have a different type of mechanical engineering, and others are

too heavy for a regular repair shop's lift system. In either case, you will not be able to simply roll your van up to any mechanic's shop for basic maintenance.

These two reasons make a compelling case for learning how to do your own basic vehicle care, such as changing oil and oil filters, as well as air filters and fuel filters. While finding a mechanic who can work on your van might be tricky, finding an auto parts store that carries the items you need is far less challenging.

Knowing your vehicle inside and out isn't entirely necessary, especially if you have a particular mechanical ineptitude; however, you will want to become familiar enough with your van to diagnose certain issues. You may want to consider a few automotive classes or online courses. You can also enhance your knowledge or learning process by checking out online videos, which you can bookmark for future reference.

Once you have learned the basic mechanical anatomy and processes of your vehicle, you will want to keep several references in your vehicle at all times. The first is the owner's manual. It can be somewhat tricky to track down owner's manuals, especially if you are purchasing an older vehicle or one that has already gone through several rounds of remodels or rehabs. However, you should be able to find supplemental information online that can provide key information on motors, as well as years, makes, and models of a variety of vehicles.

In addition to the owner's manual, you will want a repair handbook specific to your vehicle type. Understanding the basics in your vehicle could save you hundreds of dollars and days of possible lost time, simply by being able to identify where the problem is.

Lastly, you will need to keep immaculate maintenance records of your own. Not only will this help you track when you need regular preventive care, like oil changes and tire rotations, but can help you record any patterns or trouble areas, such as brakes wearing down too quickly or hoses needing replacing more frequently than you imagined.

As you learn about your vehicle, pay attention to what tools you'll need to fix common repair techniques. Often these tools will be useful for a variety of maintenance in and around the van and will become part of your onboard kit.

Your Key Equipment

While we'll discuss the type of equipment you'll need in your van further in Section 2 and 3, it is important to note that you will also be responsible for the care and maintenance of the equipment within your van.

This can include everything from your cooking surface to your water and power systems, to your most low-tech equipment, such as a cooler or tent.

When living in a van, you do not have the luxury of packing loads of supplies. Instead, you have limited space and thus need to pack only necessary gear, and tools essential for the repair of that gear. For example, instead of packing a main tent and a spare, a better use of space is to pack a tent and a tent repair kit.

You may also be limited as to what you can easily replace. Buying new screens for your windows may seem tempting, but your budget will dictate whether you can do this. Instead, consider learning how to repair the equipment that you will have onboard.

This will likely mean investing in tools and common repair elements, such as tarps, duct tape, twine, and more. As you learn how each piece of equipment in your van works, learn how it can fail to function and what you'll need to have onboard to keep it in good working order. Again, this will save you hundreds of dollars and tons of frustration.

Locations for Landing

At some point in your day, you will need to rest. Your van will also likely thank you for the break. Therefore, you will need to know where, when, and how long you can park your van in a variety of locations. After all, getting a ticket or threatened with towing will put a real damper on your experience... and budget.

Unfortunately, "free parking" is more a thing of the past in inhabited areas. Loiterers and an influx of illegal activity have really put a damper on being able to park and sleep for the night. However, there are some locations in which you'll be able to catch at least a few hours of shut-eye.

Some retail locations — especially stores that supply outdoor activities — still permit adventurers of all kinds a few hours to rest in their parking lots. Before you make assumptions, however, be sure to check with store management to understand the parameters of their offerings. Also, you'll always want to obey posted signage. Sometimes the business does not own the parking lot, so separate rules will apply to those traveling through.

Truck stops and rest areas are other popular spots for a quick rest. Again, there may be time limits on your stay. Always obey posted signs and local ordinances. These will generally be posted in a common area of the rest stop.

Another fantastic resource for free parking is National Land. This refers to land within National Forests or territory that is not otherwise owned or maintained by a private owner. The majority of this land lies west of the Mississippi River, and can be a fantastic opportunity for van people. While these are not paved or maintained sites, and they will not feature luxuries such as even the most remote vault toilet, you can find flat, remote places where you can legally park for free. Once again, there may be limits on how long you can stay in these spots.

Finding spots to park may seem like a game of roulette, but there are actually many resources available to help you hunt down options. (These have been included in the **Resource Guide** at the end of the book.) Van people are, above all, sympathetic to each others' quests and willing to help out whenever possible. Therefore, a wealth of information can be found online or even by talking to others on the road.

Van living does require knowledge and skills, beyond that which you may have at the outset of planning your new lifestyle. However, keep in mind that any lifestyle has a learning curve. When you moved into your house, for example, you probably had to learn where all the light switches were, or how to get the hot water to work. Van living is a very similar experience — you need to learn a new skill set. But once learned, it will help you immeasurably and become part of your daily rituals.

Chapter 3: The Human Element of Van Life- Health and Wealth

Besides requiring a certain amount of mechanical know-how, there are quite a few existential challenges you will encounter on the road, which require mental preparation before you embark on your new mobile lifestyle.

One thing to keep in mind is that you are by and large in control of your overall experience. Everything you have, you make happen. You will no longer have the opportunity to walk over to the neighbor's house to borrow a cup of sugar. You will need to be prepared for everything the road throws at you.

At the same time, do not be bogged down by responsibility. While van living is a totally different type of lifestyle, in time, it will become second nature. Just as you had to figure out life in your first apartment or how to adapt to your first job; you will learn to live in a van. However, be gentle with yourself and allow yourself time to get comfortable with the notion. In the early days, you may question your decision or find yourself unsure of what to do next. This is normal. We all experience growing pains and a learning curve whenever we make huge changes in our lives.

To begin, you can prepare for your new lifestyle before you even purchase your van. Not only can you learn maintenance procedures and parking regulations, but you can prepare yourself for the challenges you'll face as a human as well.

Your Health

In addition to taking care of your van and equipment, you will need to take care of yourself while you are on the road. Not only will your body need to be fed when it is hungry, have access to adequate clean water, and rest when necessary, but you will need regular maintenance as well. Staying in perfect health becomes more complicated when you are on the road. You will be exposed to a new world of germs, and you won't be able to visit your regular doctor if you start feeling under the weather.

There are many things you can do, to ensure your health is always a priority:

1. Pack a first aid kit, including care for multiple types of wounds and injuries. This includes bandages, wraps, antiseptic cream, absorbent pads, athletic wrap and tape, as well as instant ice packs and heat packs.
2. Pack a wellness kit, too. This can include cold medicine, over-the-counter products for pain and fever, topical cream for sprains and strains, throat lozenges, sleep aids, and products for heart-burn or upset stomachs.
3. Consider a daily vitamin. Even with a refrigeration system, you won't be able to have full, immediate access to all the fresh fruit and vegetables you had at home, so make sure your body and immune system are fully prepared.
4. If you are on any daily prescriptions, talk to your prescribing physician before you hit the road. You may wish to transfer your prescriptions to a national pharmacy chain and purchase prescriptions in 90-day supplies whenever possible. Often, this will require your doctor's approval. Also share with your doctor where you will be traveling, as some states do not permit non-residents to pick up certain prescriptions. You do not want

to suffer the side effects of missed essential medication while on the road, as that can quickly become serious. Planning ahead with your doctor will ensure you are ahead of the game.

5. Illness will happen. Before you hit the road, consider what your backup plan will be in case you are too sick to drive for several days. Hotels and long-term parking facilities can be expensive but may prove necessary when you are sick. The alternative of driving while you are unable has far greater consequences.

6. Consider your insurance situation, as well. What will happen if you need to go to the hospital, emergency room, or urgent care? In the United States, private insurance is often a requirement to offset very high expenses. What is your plan for carrying insurance during your travels?

Mental Wellness

In addition to your physical well-being, consider your mental health, as well. Being on the road is not always fun! The road will bring more rewards than regrets, but there will be days when you are stationary because of maintenance, sickness, or complacency. There will be days when you "just don't wanna." If you have a "go, go, go" type of plan, there may come a time when you want to "rest, rest, rest." You will need to listen to your mind and body when these days happen because your health is always going to be a huge factor in your overall success on the road.

What will you do when the weather is bad? You might have a day of hiking washed out by unexpected thunderstorms. You may plan to do some maintenance but find yourself unable to do so on a foggy day. Things will not always go as planned, and sometimes the impeding factor is the weather itself. You will likely not want to spend the day confined in your van, which means you'll need to learn how to play along with Mother Nature. Not only will you need a solid weather app, but weather gear, as well. There are certain points in the United States where snow exists year-round. There are also locations where the temperatures can reach over 100 degrees.

Besides being prepared with equipment, make sure you're mentally ready for bad weather, too. If it's going to rain, perhaps you find a local, free museum. If the temperatures are going to be incredibly high, sleep during the day and drive at night to avoid overheating yourself and your van.

Additionally, boredom is real. Finding structure will help you prevent this, but it's going to happen. You might have a daily ritual, but even that will become tedious at times. Even when you find yourself driving to your next adventure, you might find yourself sick of driving and tired of listening to the same old music. This is natural. Don't take boredom as a sign of failure. Instead, pull over and find a new station, podcast, or audiobook. Perhaps you can take some time to catch up on your housekeeping and organization. Maybe you pause and write down how you're feeling. Do a search online for somewhere nearby to take a stroll and clear your thoughts.

When you feel this way at home, what do you do? Most likely, you throw on some television, or call your friends, or find something around the house to occupy your time. You can still do these things on the road, too! It's entirely ok to feel burnt out on driving all the time. Allow yourself downtime, and when you find yourself feeling bored of that, seek out new ways to occupy your time. Consider picking up games and activity books or coloring books. What about journaling? If you're a creator, you can still paint, knit, and craft on the road, or dabble in whatever your preferred media is. Anything you can do to occupy your time can be done in a van, as long as you're willing to change the scale. For example, you won't be able to throw an entire pottery wheel and kiln on your van, but you can grab some modeling clay and play with making tiny creations that will exercise your talent and creativity.

Your Wealth

Despite not having fixed bills, van living can be expensive. Prepare for this now. Before you start budgeting — which we'll discuss in another section — you need to know what types of expenses you can encounter. This includes everything from mechanical breakdowns and flat tires, to daily expenses, like gasoline, food, water, and generator operation. Parking permits cost money, and showering on the road can cost money too (if you don't have a water supply onboard). Every cup of coffee you purchase at a gas station dips into your budget.

If you plan to make van living your full-time lifestyle, what will you do for income? Many employers offer the opportunity to work remotely, which can be a huge benefit, depending on your profession. This also means you'll likely need to be sure you have a functioning laptop and a reliable Wi-Fi signal. While more and more public locations offer free Wi-Fi, consider if you'll really want to spend every day in a new coffee shop or home improvement store parking lot borrowing signal in order to send in a big report. Instead, you may wish to invest in a web connection amplifier or booster, so that you can run your office right from your van.

You may instead decide to do freelance work on the road. You'll be surrounded by infinite muses, so if you are able to do so, make it happen! You can also run a blog or livestream your journey. Again, this will require a Wi-Fi signal and likely a handful of equipment, so be sure you have a solid plan in place before you set up your van. Having an adequate workspace in your van will definitely increase your professional success.

Van living is incredibly rewarding; however, it does include a bit of adaptation, especially if you've lived a relatively sedentary, domestic life. You may feel like a proverbial fish out of water for some time, but this does not mean you're "doing it wrong." In fact, it means you're finally spreading your wings and finding your groove.

Advice from The Road- Part 1

I hate to be the bearer of bad news, but everything is going to go wrong. Not necessarily all at once, but don't rule that out!

When we hit the road, we started slowly. We started with a two week trip around the vicinity of our home. We wanted to make sure that, no matter what happened, we would be within a reasonable distance of our actual home, so we could "come back" if everything proved to be too much. That included too expensive, too scary, too unpredictable... if at any point we got overwhelmed, we could dart back home and say we had a very nice, short vacation.

Everything went according to plan. We saw the sights, we took the back roads, we gathered loads of amazing photographs and memories. Then, just nine hours away from home, everything went sideways. Huge mechanical breakdown — one of those situations where one thing breaks, and then all the bits and pieces around it start breaking. It was beyond anything we could take care of ourselves because so many things were just falling apart.

Worse yet — we were supposed to be in a wedding at home in just two days!

We had the choice of trying to find someone who could help fix it, or just abandon our van, find a rental car, and figure out how to get the van back later. It took all day, but we were able to find — and get the van to — a mechanic. Even then, it wasn't fixable without ordering parts that would take several days to arrive.

Thankfully, the mechanic was sympathetic to van life. He'd done it himself. Since he couldn't fix it, he came up with a suitable workaround that would get us home. He also recommended that, once we started driving, we not stop except for fuel.

We thought we were home free but still fell prey to the mayhem that can be road life. Even when you think things are going well, it just takes one situation to remind you that "fine" is a temporary state of mind.

Still, there's nothing I'd give up about life on the road. Bad things happen in an apartment. Your car can break down on the way to the office. Your milk will go bad, and your dog will barf in your shoes.

A Van Lifer is someone who can adapt, overcome, and think of creative situations to nearly every problem. Furthermore, they accept that sometimes the solution is "ask an expert." Van Life is a community effort, even if that community is constantly moving in different directions!

Did we get back on the road? Absolutely! We had to spend a bit more time at home than we planned, getting the parts we needed, but that gave us time to learn more about the situation and research solutions for when (not if) it happened again.

Section 2: Finding Your New Home

Being aware of what it takes to successfully live on the road is all well and good, but once you have your mind made up, it's time to find the chariot that will carry you through all of life's adventures.

Again, you might take to the internet to find pictures of vans with white-washed walls, gleaming hardwood floors, tile backsplashes, and even wood-burning stoves. Looks awfully cozy, doesn't it?

While you can make these beautiful images part of your reality, the truth is that it will take a lot of work to get there.

In this section, we'll look at the different things you need to keep in mind when choosing your new vehicle, as well as how to proceed with converting your van into your dream home.

Chapter 1: Considerations for Choosing the Right Vehicle

If you look at any Van Life-themed social media account, you'll find that the term "van" is somewhat open to interpretation. You'll see a fair share of classic vans, such as Volkswagen Vanagons, Westphalia, and Transporters. You'll also see conversion vans, cargo vans, and European camper vans. But the lifestyle also extends to "skoolies," or converted school buses. This, in turn, has inspired folks to convert buses of all kinds. Inventive folks have also taken to converting campers from part-time vacation homes to full-time homes on wheels.

So, when you start searching for your new home, you might be completely stalled at how many options are available. In a nutshell, your decision will be driven by a lot of personal factors. Let's examine these further.

Determining Vehicle Size

There's a considerable amount of difference in size between a skoolie and a VW Transporter, just as there's a huge difference between a three-bed-room house and a studio apartment.

One of the first things you'll need to consider is how much space you need. There are a lot of elements that can go into this part of your accommodations.

1. The number of passengers — and their species!
2. The length of the trip
3. The amenities, such as a bathroom, food preparation area, etc
4. Personal preference

The number of passengers will, of course, dictate how many seats and how many sleeping areas you will need in your van. If you'll have children with you, you might feel most comfortable if they're able to be safely belted into fixed seats while the vehicle is moving. While nearly every veteran van lifer has an amusing story of using a cooler as a seat, it's frowned upon by the law and definitely not safe!

If you're bringing your Adventure Pup or a Feline Mascot (neither of which is unheard of!), you'll have to plan to accommodate their needs, as well. For dogs, you'll want to make sure you have room for them to rest while you drive, move around as they wish when they're not on an adventure with you, and a spot for them to sleep. This can mean making room for a dog bed or making room in your bed for a dog. Cats typically need around 16-18 square feet of space to feel comfortable. They'll also need a litter pan that won't slosh all over the floor of the van unless otherwise toilet trained. Many people do share their van life with a furry friend, so it can be done, with careful planning!

The second part of determining space from the number of passengers is based on comfort level. If you are currently sharing a three-bedroom house with two children and a dog, You're accustomed to a certain amount of space in which to maneuver. Even in the largest bus, you will still run into each other, and you will find privacy a very rare element, indeed. However, if you're currently sharing a studio with your partner, then you're already well-prepared for the challenges that come with cohabitating in a tiny space.

The length of the trip will also dictate the size of vehicle you need, if largely from the standpoint of accommodating four seasons worth of equipment and clothing. If you plan on making your van your permanent home, then you'll need to consider how you'll plan for the seasonal changes. Perhaps you take the opportunity to "chase the weather" and always park somewhere where the weather is dry and warm. Perhaps you choose a vehicle with additional storage for rain gear, snow gear, heavier blankets or sleeping bags, and fans for hot weather.

If you have the opportunity to stop and regroup periodically through your trip, you won't need to stash as much stuff. If you have a small storage unit (or a friend or relative who's willing to let you borrow some space), you can swing by as the situation calls for to change out your equipment, clothing, and more. Granted, this means you'll have to plan ahead to drive to that specific location in time, but it can save you hundreds of pounds and several square feet of extra "stuff" you don't need to carry with you everywhere.

The next consideration is how you will use the room within your vehicle. If you plan to have a bathroom area, you're likely going to want a camper- or bus-type set up. If you instead plan to pack a portable toilet and bucket-style shower, you can really make any type of vehicle work. We'll discuss this in more detail shortly, but at this stage, you'll want to consider if you want to have a full water closet with plumbing or if you can deal with an alternative plan.

The same is true for food preparation areas. The most rugged vans might have a cooler and a propane burner. The most luxurious have full oven ranges, small refrigerators, kitchen sinks, and cabinets. In between are an almost infinite variety of choices. We'll discuss kitchen needs and practical applications in a later section too, but at this stage, consider how much room you feel will be necessary for the kind of food prep you plan. If you're going to install plumbing, gas, or electricity for this, it's best to think of it now.

Lastly, your own personal preferences are something you truly need to consider. On paper, a solo voyager needs only a driver's seat and a bed, with room for storage. In reality, you might find yourself feeling very claustrophobic. The opposite can be true, too. You might find yourself overwhelmed by the size of your space and the maintenance required to keep it clean and functional.

One practical test that is recommended by all sorts of van life experts is the "try it at home" test. Before purchasing a van, bus, or camper of any kind, look up the approximate dimensions of space within the vehicle. Next, find a space in your home, garage, yard, basement, etc., and tape off those exact dimensions. Some experts recommend hanging sheets or shower curtains to give the illusion of the van walls, but you may be able to get a feel for what you'll be working with without going that far.

Without anything in it, how does this space feel? Now start adding objects to the area, either figuratively by marking off the space with tape or chalk, or literally. How big is the sleeping area? If you take that portion away, how well can you maneuver in the remaining space? There will be a learning curve when you actually start living in a van, but if you feel uncomfortable with the space before it's even "real," then you'll definitely want to consider a different option.

Another thing to keep in mind is the height of the van. If you're going with a regular-style van that does not have a pop-top, you may not be able to stand fully upright in the back. For those who are planning to use the van only as a place to sleep and store things, this might be perfectly acceptable. For others, this might be extremely limiting. Again, this comes down to personal preference, but it is definitely something you'll want to consider before you invest in your new home on wheels.

Vehicle Specifications
Beyond the considerations of space, there is the fact that you will have to drive this vehicle from time to time!

Of course, size is a consideration when operating a vehicle, as well. You should feel comfortable driving your van, camper, or bus in a variety of conditions, including on regular city streets, on the highway, on unmaintained or unpaved roads, and also be able to park and reverse.

While your particular trip might not include all of these elements, there will be times when something unforeseen occurs, and you'll need to make do. For example, there are parts of the country where the detour for a temporarily closed well-traveled road is a dirt path. Additionally, you might find it necessary to hit the freeway to get to the next closest gas station, even if you've carefully planned to avoid cities as much as possible. Therefore, it's important to be able to safely guide your vehicle wherever you happen to roam.

If you plan to frequently encounter those unmaintained and unpaved roads, you'll also want to pay close attention to your drivetrain. A drivetrain contains the parts (components) of a vehicle that deliver power to certain wheels.

Let's look at the differences:

- Two-wheel drive (2WD). If your van is referred to as "rear-wheel drive" or "front-wheel drive," it's a 2WD model.
    - Rear-wheel drive delivers the power to the back wheels, and thus the vehicle is "pushed" forward from behind, so the front wheels can handle steering. Many sports cars are RWD, resulting in a balanced, powerful drive. On the flip side, RWD vehicles perform poorly in wet or freezing conditions.
    - Front-wheel drive delivers power to the front wheels, where the engine weight provides balance that improves overall traction. These vehicles typically have a more respectable fuel economy, as well, which can be important to your budget.

- Four-wheel drive (4WD). This option allows drivers to select between RWD and 4WD, depending on the terrain. 4WD delivers power to all four wheels simultaneously, which is fantastic when taking on tough terrain but terrible for your fuel economy. This is why engineers offer the ability to turn off 4WD when the conditions don't require it.
- All-wheel drive (AWD). This option is becoming more and more popular with larger vehicles. AWD requires a front, rear, and central differential, which means all four wheels have power when they need it. A lot of modern (post-2015) heavy-duty vehicles offer this type of drivetrain as an option. Automatic AWD operates in 2WD until the computer sensors determine extra power is needed in a specific location. It is unlikely that you will find this feature on a bus or older van, however.

The rest of the vehicle options you'll need to choose between are far more intuitive. Do you want an engine that runs on regular gasoline or diesel? Check the specifications for any vehicle you're interested in to determine what kind of fuel it needs, as well as the overall fuel economy.

What about transmission? Can you drive a standard, or will an automatic transmission be the best option for you and any others who will be along for the trip? While fans of each option can debate the merits and downfalls of each for eternity, the reality, in this case, is that you'll need to be able to choose a van you can regularly drive without issue.

Insurance

We won't go into too much detail on this topic because requirements and options vary from state to state and country to country. Still, insurance is a very important part of the equation. Not only will you need to have insurance on your vehicle if you plan to drive anywhere, but you'll want to make sure your contents are covered, as well.

Before you purchase any van, bus, or camper, speak with your insurance representative. You'll want to make sure you're covered not only as a driver but also for any accidents that might befall your new home. There are plenty of situations that might render your vehicle undrivable or your quarters unliveable. You need to make sure you're protected not just on the road but for your lifestyle, as well.

When you speak to your insurance representative, make sure you bring up all of these concerns and receive a quote. You will need to decide if you prefer to budget for a higher level of insurance coverage or put away enough savings as a cushion for any mishaps that occur. While it may seem early to think about this, it's crucial that you are able to afford the insurance on any vehicle you might take out on the road. Otherwise, it's simply not the vehicle for you!

Chapter 2: So Many Choices!

If you were to type the word "van" into Google, you'd probably get far, far more information than you could rationally digest in one sitting. Therefore, we'll quickly run through the different types of vehicles you might consider, as well as some factors that might go into your decision to purchase — or stay far away from — that type.

There are plenty of nuances and adaptations to each and every individual van, so it would be impossible to review every single brand that has ever been used for van life. Instead, we'll look at the overall classes of van, and remember — these are just basic guidelines. As they say on the road, "Your Mileage May Vary!"

Classic Vans

These are your Vanagons, your Westphalia, Transporters, and all of the Instagram-ready VW campers that fit the expected stereotype. This class can also include any pre-1990 vans from any manufacturer.

Speaking from an aesthetic point of view, these vehicles are often very photogenic and will get tons of attention on the road. They've got that "old school" appeal that dredges up pleasant, nostalgic memories in nearly anyone who traveled extensively in childhood.

There is, in fact, a huge community of Classic Van Lifers, so you'll be able to connect with plenty of folks who have extensively driven, maintained, rehabbed, worked on, lived in, or are in any possible way familiar with these vans. This is great news for anyone new to van life because you'll have plenty of resources and support through each step of the process.

In fact, when shopping for a Classic Van, you'll find that a large portion of those for sale will be more or less road-ready, due to the fact that many people have purchased and rehabbed these vehicles, then moved on to a bigger and better project following the success of their maiden voyage.

Also, thanks to the recent resurgence in popularity of these vehicles, it's not too difficult to find information that will guide you through basic repairs and maintenance. Since these are vehicles that are actually driven on the road regularly today, it's not too terribly hard to find spare parts, either.

Being able to handle repairs and find spare parts easily is a good thing because you will likely have to do this with frequency, unfortunately. Older vehicles, no matter how well maintained, are prone to breakdowns. Hoses wear out, parts get bent, you might run too hot or too cold, and things will simply stop working over time. If you choose an older vehicle like a Classic Van, try to get as complete a service history as possible. You might also luck out and find one with a new or refurbished engine, but always inspect all of the mechanical aspects — you never know when one of them is going to show their age.

Another consideration is the maintenance you can't handle on your own. Some of the older, foreign-built vehicles require special tools, parts, or mechanical knowledge. Rather than being able to breeze into any auto mechanic's garage, you will need to make sure someone on staff can repair your year, make, and model of van. A breakdown is always inconvenient, but extra frustrating when you have to spend time and energy figuring out where to go for assistance.

Additionally, things like "fuel efficiency" and "safety technology" are relatively new terms in the automotive world. Unlike today's vehicles, the vans of the 1960s didn't need to meet speed limits of 70 miles per hour regularly. Seatbelts didn't become mandatory until 1968. Airbags didn't become a requirement until 1998. Though Classic Vans are built like actual tanks in many regards, they are — by and large — lacking in the modern technology of current vehicles.

Conversion Vans

A Conversion Van is a type of van that is able to "convert" to a livable space. Early conversion vans of the 1970s simply added extra seating, or seats that folded into beds, and plush features, like carpeting and interior lighting. In the 1980s and 90s, features like televisions, VCRs, and indoor-style outlets were added to the category. Conversion vans are insulated, ventilated, and may be equipped with an isolated battery for a non-engine power source. In many ways, conversion vans are not unlike some of today's standard SUVs. But, even the most well-equipped conversion van will require some adaptation in order to be a full-time home.

Conversion vans are typically not too terribly expensive to purchase or maintain. It's relatively easy to find an older Chevy, Ford, or Dodge conversion van that has decent bones at a decent price. Since these vans are usually based on, very similar to, or completely identical to regular passenger vans, it's easy to find parts, and you won't need to find a mechanic who specializes in your particular van.

Spending less on the vehicle itself means you can allocate more funds toward the customization of the vehicle. It's also very likely that you'll find a Conversion Van that has some of the parts and pieces that you'll want in your finished van. For example, a lot of Conversion Vans have out-ward-swinging doors instead of sliding doors. Many manufacturers use this option as a way to stash fold-out tables or storage, which you can incorporate into your overall van scheme. Many also have built-in storage, which you can expand upon or leave as-is. You'll be able to enjoy seats with seatbelts that then fold into beds, saving you the problem of seats and beds as separate entities.

Some Conversion Vans were created with higher roofs, which may allow you to stand up comfortably but will definitely let you take advantage of more storage opportunities along the walls or roof.

Cargo Vans

Cargo Vans share the same advantages as Conversion Vans when it comes to being regularly maintained. Cargo Vans are being manufactured to this day, often as part of vehicle fleets for commercial and industrial businesses. Typically, Cargo Vans have a completely empty body, aside from a driver and passenger seat. Some have old tool racks, storage cabinets, or hanging storage in the back, depending on what they were used for in their past life. You may choose to incorporate or remove these to start fresh.

One thing that many Van Lifers enjoy about Cargo Vans is that they have very few windows. That means any wall is appropriate for building or storing. That also means you don't have to worry about looky-loos peeping in your van when it's parked or while you're sleeping.

On the flip side, both cargo and conversion vans typically have a lower fuel economy. While most options will function on regular unleaded gasoline, which tends to be less expensive, you will be stopping at fuel stations more regularly. You may also wish to keep spare fuel on hand for emergency situations.

You might find that many of the cargo vans on the market have very high mileage, especially if they were regularly used as part of a business. The advantage to this is that business vehicles are usually well-maintained since they're a crucial part of the operation. Still, you'll want to be prepared for any aging vehicle maintenance requirements that might come up.

Depending on your willingness to invest time and money into the van project, having no basic setup in a cargo van might also be a disadvantage. After all, you will need to create a liveable space out of nothing. You can find rehabbed cargo vans for sale, but these will cost more than a completely blank slate, of course. We'll talk more about what it takes to rehab and fully construct a living space in a van in the next chapter, but this is definitely something to keep in mind at this stage of the game, as well.

Euro Vans

First, bear in mind that the term "Euro Van" can refer to two different things. First, a Volkswagen Eurovan is a very specific make and model of van. These pop-top vans were offered in the US between 1993 and 2003, and many are still around and functional today.

There are others who refer to any European touring-style van as a "Euro Van." This can include Mercedes Sprinters, Klassen vans, Fiat Ducato, Renault Trafic, and other vehicles manufactured overseas. With the exception of the Mercedes Sprinter, it's not often you'll find these types of vans in the United States; however, with the growing market for off-grid options, more and more are arriving stateside.

When you're shopping for anything under the umbrella of "Euro Van," double-check if it's an actual VW Eurovan or a European van conversion.

Interestingly enough, VW Eurovans and Sprinter vans share a lot of common features. For example, they both are designed with large and small cargo storage options. They're more modern vehicles, which means you don't have to dredge up historical data to learn more about how they work. Additionally, as modern vehicles, they're equipped with smaller engines that are more powerful and consume less fuel.

Of course, there's a downside to this: as European creations, you'll need to find a mechanic who understands the engineering. They can also be difficult to find parts for, and expensive to repair. There will be more technical elements, such as computer systems, while the earlier and older models have more manual aspects.

Additionally, one thing to keep in mind about these taller vehicles is that you will need greater clearance. While this is typically not a problem on well-traveled highways, where semis and commuter buses are expected, this may pose a challenge on some of the more off-the-beaten-path locations you wish to visit. You can also encounter issues with parking garages if you find yourself within city limits.

Buses

There is a lot that can be said about buses, but the three basic options are School Bus, Coach, or Transit. Though the term "Skoolie" refers specifically to School Buses, the community as a whole tends to accept nearly any bus under the umbrella term.

There are significant differences between the three. True Skoolies are very affordable. Retired school buses can be acquired from multiple sources, including junkyard auctions, school district dispersal sales, online auctions, and more. There are several different lengths and configurations available as well.

Coach buses are bigger and bulkier than school buses, but they have one significant advantage: Uunder-cabin storage. If you've ever traveled the country by bus, you'll recall stowing your bags under the bus at the curb. This is great if you want to take along bicycles or large gear, or need to pack for all seasons. The size of the vehicle can be somewhat daunting though when navigating narrow city streets or winding mountain passages.

Transit buses are retired city buses. Like skoolies, these can come in various shapes and sizes. They rarely have the extra storage, but one unique feature is that some smaller city buses are equipped with wheelchair lifts or entry-assist options, which can be very helpful for those with mobility concerns.

Nearly all buses are equipped with a diesel engine, but some will have the engine in front, while others have the engine in the rear. If you're planning on running plumbing and electric wiring, you'll definitely need to mind the engine. You'll also need to know how to access it for repairs and maintenance, and pack the essential equipment, including any ladders or hydraulic lifts you might need.

One major downside to buses is that repair shops are extremely scarce for these vehicles. They tend to be pretty straightforward in their engineering, so it is possible to learn some DIY repair techniques, but if you're not mechanically inclined, you might have a rough time in the event of a breakdown.

Additionally, insurance can be a bit tricky on buses, but not impossible. As mentioned before, speak to your local representative to get the details before you go on a bus buying spree!

Campers

"Campers" is another somewhat ambiguous term. Some people call any van that you can sleep in a "camper." Others consider pull-behind trailers with living quarters "campers." For some, a "camper" is a full RV. Still others consider a "camper" a trailer that contains nothing more than room to sleep and adequate ventilation and weather protection.

There's a huge difference between an Airstream "camper" and a Patriot "camper" and a Vistabule "camper." When searching and shopping, be fully aware of what anything under the generic term "camper" entails.

For the most part, anything with the title of "camper" will be a prefabricated home on the road. It will include sleep areas, food prep areas, seating areas, and storage. There may be a bathroom, depending on the size of the camper. It may be a trailer instead of a combined living/driving space, such as in a van or a bus. Then again, one man's trailer is another man's camper!

When it comes to choosing the type of vehicle you plan to take on the road, there are really no "wrong" answers. While every class of vehicle has its own community that is completely devoted to that particular model, there are advantages and disadvantages to every single one. You'll find that even within these communities, there will be devotees to a certain year, make, or model.

Therefore, it's really impractical to listen to the recommendations of online forums, friends, or family members unless they face the same exact challenges, situations, and preferences as you will. Instead, pay attention to details. What are the dimensions? How many seats? What kind of engine does it have? What does its maintenance history look like? What type of fuel economy does it get? And most importantly — are you going to feel comfortable living in it?

Chapter 3: Ready-to-Roll, or Ready-to-Rehab?

The next consideration for your van home is how much work you want to put into transforming the space inside into the home of your dreams.

Ask yourself these two questions:

Do you want to create the ultimate space, in which you can comfortably live the rest of your life?

More importantly, are you willing to put in months or even years of hard work in order to create that space?

When asked what was most surprising about the process of gutting and rehabbing a van or bus, nearly everyone who has gone through the exercise will say the time of the entire process. When you browse those gorgeous van homes on the internet, see if you can't research the owners or builders to see how long they spent on the process. Many are very upfront with the process of refurnishing it, including all of the challenges that go along with that. After all, Van Life is a community effort!

Though many of the vans and skoolies you see on social media are labors of love, rebuilt from bare bones, you can start with a fully ready-to-roll vehicle. Yes, it will cost you more at the outset, but buying a fully rehabbed and refurbed vehicle means you won't have to strip the inside. You won't have to rewire anything. You won't have to learn practical plumbing. You won't have to create structures. You won't have to source lumber, nails, screws, tools, hinges... nothing! You can simply open the doors to your new home, look around, and decide where you want to put your belongings.

If that sounds like an absolute nightmare, then you are clearly more in the "Do It Yourself" camp. Before you purchase a giant transit bus and start demolition, there are a few things you need to ask yourself:

How much time can you devote each day to construction?
For many, construction starts out as a "little bit each day" type of project, but swiftly becomes a full obsession. There will be setbacks. Things will not work out exactly as planned. You will cut a piece of insulation multiple times, trying to get it to fit along a curved wall... and eventually, you will cut it to the point where you can't use it. You will find that the plumbing absolutely cannot go there, or there, or really anywhere that it might make sense. Every person who has ever changed anything about their van has been in this exact position.

And that is how we become obsessed — this drive to solve all problems immediately takes over all reason. At the same time, you might still be working your day job as you work on your van space. Your partner, your children, your dog and cat, might all be rightfully concerned that you're spending all night in the van.

This is an easy way to burn yourself out on the whole project. As you encounter one frustration after another, you might decide it's not worth it. While we have no practical cures for the difficulties you'll no doubt encounter, it is highly recommended that you work on your van or bus slowly and surely, rather than trying to rush through it. If you're planning a very extensive makeover, don't plan to leave in two months.
A simple rule of thumb: If time is of the essence, choose something that's ready to go (or at least very close). If you want to really create something from the ground up, don't have a deadline.

Can You Build It?

Be very honest with yourself: do you know anything about construction, electricity, plumbing, insulation, drywall, cabinetry, etc.? Or, are you handy enough that you feel very confident about learning? Can you see a straight line, take a variety of accurate measurements, and execute the product in your mind?

There are four main steps to the process of creating your dream space inside a van.

First, you need to gut it. This is especially true if you purchase a bus that still has the seats inside. You will need to remove everything, and you will need to somehow get rid of it or repurpose it.

As a side note, you will need to be creative when it comes to the collection of school bus seats you're about to have if you've gone with a skoolie. Some folks have luck selling them "as is" to people in the area or via online auctions. More likely, you'll want to take them apart and sell the metal for scrap. Unless you have loads of space in which to store dozens of seats, this is something you ought to plan on doing before you bring your skoolie home, too.

Once you've got your open space, you need a functional design. You'll need to consider not just the overall flow, but where you're going to put the heaviest weight loads, where you're going to put storage or built-ins, and the reality of where you can put plumbing or electricity, which might be based on where you put the water source or hook up, generator, or solar panels. You'll need to be aware of where and how the doors open, as well as the windows.

Most people who have completely gutted and refurbished a van report having at least two to three versions of their design plans, so don't be too concerned if your first plan has to be scrapped. Learn, and move on.

Next comes executing the design. You'll need to run any electric and plumbing before you put in insulation and walls. You'll have to put in walls before you build structures, such as cabinets, seating areas, or sleeping areas.

A side note about storage: One of the best ways to maximize storage is to put it under seating or sleeping areas. One very popular trick is to raise the sleeping area as high as you can, to create a larger storage space beneath. You can build the frame of your bed over a cabinet system to create both open and closed storage underneath your bed. Perhaps you add a fold-out table to the base of your bed or seating that pulls out like a drawer. The options are infinite!

As you are constructing your new home, you will need both materials and tools. Of the two, the tools might be the most cost-prohibitive, as well as the hardest to source. You will also make multiple trips to the hardware store each week. Therefore, you must account in your budget for tools, supplies, as well as gas money and time spent at the hardware store acquiring these things. You might see if there is a tool-lending program in your community, as this can save you several hundred dollars. You might also cruise local selling walls to see if there are used tools available in your area. The unfortunate truth about these processes though, is that you might not find what you need exactly when you need it.

Despite all of your best intentions, there will be waste. Anything from bent nails to stripped screws, to perfectly usable lumber cut to the wrong length. You will not want to keep this waste forever, so consider a plan that will allow you to collect, remove, and appropriately dispose of it. This may mean a call to a junkyard or working with your regular waste management company.

Can You Afford It?

The cost figures for fully renovating a skoolie range from $10,000 to $30,000. Granted, that's cost over time, and as mentioned earlier, it can take years to fully construct the space of your dreams.

We've alluded to some of the expenses here, but let's put it all on the table.

You'll need:

- tools
- safety equipment, such as goggles and gloves
- lumber
- screws, nails, hinges, knobs, sliding rails, bolts, and anchors
- wiring
- insulation
- plugs and switches
- pipes
- walls
- countertops/ sealed surfaces
- flooring
- faucets and fixtures for water closet

This doesn't include any decorative items, such as backsplashes or paint, or power and water supplies, which we'll discuss in more detail in the next chapter. It also doesn't include any books, courses, or instruction you might pay for to help you with your endeavors.

Do You Have the Work Space?

If you're going to be working on a vehicle for months or years, you need a space where you can safely and legally do so.

It is unlikely that a skoolie will fit in the garage of your suburban home. It is also unlikely that you'll be permitted to work extensively on demo and re-hab in the parking garage of a city condo building. If you know someone who has a large yard where you can work, that might be a great option... until the neighbors call the city.

There are legal considerations for working on vehicles within some city or corporation limits. Even if you're not disposing of harmful liquids, less enthusiastic neighbors might consider your activities a nuisance. Therefore, you'll want to find a nice, large space — preferably indoors — where you can work on your vehicle. And then a backup location. And possibly even a backup to the backup. Whether you wear out your welcome or simply outgrow your space, you'll need a plan, since you can't just plop a large bus or very tall van down anywhere.

Most beginner van projects are somewhere in between "completely ready" and "completely reconstructed." You might choose a "mostly ready" van, and lift the bed to add storage or shorten the sleeping area to add a food prep area. You might start with only the minimal changes, then add a little room here or include a fold-out table there as you spend time living in your new space.

Alternatively, you might feel that life on the road is not complete unless you have a wood-burning stove, fully functional skylights, and a hand-painted porcelain backsplash in the bathroom. There's nothing wrong with this perspective, either.

Ultimately, creating your van space is a balance between what you *want* to do, and what you *can* do. If there is a significant overlap between the two, then best wishes on your rehab and refurb experience! If you find that you're lacking in time, skill, funds, or space, you might scale back your project. You might wish to find a mostly-ready van or add the assistance of a professional if the issue is time or skill.

The internet is full of experiences shared by those who have made this journey before. We'll share a few links in the **resources guide** to get you started. When it comes to the building stage, however, you truly cannot research too much, especially if you are a novice DIY-er. You'll want to consider safety, practicality, usability, and durability of everything you construct to be 100% sure before you lay the first nail or cut the first board!

And most of all, have patience and faith. Whether or not it turns out exactly as you dreamed, it will turn out exactly as you have built it. Your planning and patience will pay off in the end.

Chapter 4: Budget Considerations for Creating Your Van

While it may seem that we harp and harp on the concept of budget, you'll find that this is with good reason. One of the most common reasons people give up on the van life dream is because they run out of money before they even have the chance to hit the road.

While it's true that you can save quite a bit of money by abandoning regular bills, multiple car payments, mortgages, and the like with the vagabond lifestyle of the road, you will need to invest a bit of money into setting up the lifestyle to be sustainable.

For those who feel cooped up, you might be so passionately drawn to the experience that you feel like you could simply hop in any old van and drive off and "make it work." There is a very specific demographic for whom this is true. If you have plenty of money, the ability to take on any odd jobs no matter where you are, no particular preference about where you sleep at night, a decent cooler, and a reliable propane burner, then it is possible to "make it work."

If you have a family, pets, the desire to have a predictable shower and bathroom experience, the ability to prepare a variety of fresh foods, and the need to sleep in a comfortable bed, then you will need to plan very carefully in the early stages.

So, when it comes to budgeting, we started at the overall "big picture" of all of the various categories of expenses that might come into play. Now it's time to start drilling down into more detail, starting with the van itself.

How Much Will It Cost to Hit the Road?

The equation for determining the overall cost of your van is as follows:

Cost of Vehicle + Cost of Repairs/Rehab/Refurb = Pre-Road Cost

(Cost of oil/oil change x 6) + cost of tires + cost for replacement cost + hourly rate for emergency maintenance = Annual Upkeep Cost

Size of fuel tank x Average Miles Per Gallon = Miles Per Tank
Total Distance Traveled (divided by) Miles Per Tank = Total Number of Fuel Stops
(Size of fuel tank x going rate for fuel) x Number of Fuel Stops = Total Fuel Budget

Pre-Road Cost + Annual Upkeep Cost + Total Fuel Budget is the amount you will need to get you through the first year on the road.

There are ways to maximize your money, however.

First, remember that the bigger the vehicle, the more fuel it will need. Consider purchasing the smallest possible van or bus that you can actually live in. This might require you to do the "try it at home" test a few times with different configurations.

In addition, consider planning your wandering strategically. Instead of California one week and Connecticut the next, consider taking some time to wind along the West Coast. Try finding a good central location where you can park for a longer period of time, and use a bicycle or small motorbike or scooter to explore the sights nearby. This will not only save fuel costs but wear and tear costs on your van as a whole, minimizing maintenance costs. Lastly, if you find a free spot to camp within National Lands, you'll save a significant amount of money on camp fees and site fees while you do this exploration. Another thing to keep in mind when looking at the annual budget is your income. We'll discuss working from the road in more detail shortly, but there are ways to make money while you travel. Any income you make will offset your expenses, of course, and can either go toward regular maintenance and fuel or toward an emergency fund.

Power and Water: The Utilities

There are also some features you can add to the van construction that will help you save, as well. If you add a power supply and water supply, you'll have a fully self-sustaining home on wheels. This means you'll have a lower reliance on stopping at full-service camping parks. You'll be able to produce the power to charge your phones and devices, as well as have a functioning bathroom to help with showers and general clean up.

When it comes to power supplies, the top two options are generators and solar power. Each option has, of course, strong arguments for and against them.

First, let's look at generators:

Pros	Cons
Produce a lot of instant power at any time	Noisy
Not weather dependent	Require fuel and ongoing maintenance
Can handle a lot of wattage	May be prohibited in some locations due to fumes

Now let's look at the argument surrounding solar power:

Pros	Cons
No fumes, no noise, no maintenance	Does not create a lot of power
Can be repositioned as necessary	Power supply is dependent upon intake/positioning
No on-going expenses: install and done	Can be damaged, which requires replacement

All said, it boils down to your personal preference and budget. A generator will be an ongoing expense but will be able to supply great quantities of instant power. This might be a greater advantage than disadvantage if you're going to need to power a laptop, phone, and WiFi hotspot. On the other hand, if you won't need tons of power all the time, solar panels might be a real budget-saving option.

There are Van Lifers who live without power. You can choose this route as well. Between independent battery charge units, USB plugs in more modern vehicles, and the old-fashioned type of plug that uses a decommissioned cigarette lighter port, it's possible to keep a cell phone charged. You can also take breaks at fast food restaurants, rest stations, or laundromats, and mooch a little power while you fuel your own body, shower, or catch up on some laundry. Before you help yourself to some power, make sure it's allowed. It also probably goes without saying, but never leave your phone unattended, as it will very likely take a voyage of its own. And if you're going to borrow a little electricity, it's considered good road manners if you make a purchase while you're there.

The next consideration is the water supply. If you are going to carry your own water supply, you'll need two tanks — one for freshwater, and one for greywater. Most experts recommend each tank hold up to 5-7 gallons. The main factor in deciding how big of a tank you want is how much you can carry yourself, as you'll be responsible for filling, maintaining, and emptying these tanks. One gallon of water weighs approximately 8 pounds, for reference. Therefore, a five-gallon tank will be a heft of close to 50 pounds, once you include the weight of the tank itself.

You'll also want to make sure that any tank, pipes, or tubing involved with your freshwater supply is FDA-rated as food safe.

Greywater tanks do not have to be food-safe, but are just as important. "Greywater" refers to wastewater from your sink, shower, etc.

You'll want to make sure that both your freshwater and greywater tanks are both accessible and secured, so they are equally available for filling and emptying, and don't slosh around while you drive.

If you're looking for a very simple way to access freshwater, consider the gravity method. This basically involves installing the water supply in a way that gravity delivers the water through the tubing, to your waiting hands, cup, bucket, or wherever you need the water to go. Many rudimentary van shower systems use this method by hanging the water supply over a door or from an overhead hook, and releasing a valve so the water flows freely.

For those who wish to have more control over water flow, a manual hand or foot pump can be installed. Hand pumps require very little mechanical know-how and involve a temporary or fixed pump being added to the open end of the freshwater tank. The design is not unlike a soap or lotion bottle pump dispenser, only on a larger scale. Foot pumps will require a directed flow via a faucet and sink so that the greywater tank catches the runoff and waste, but they offer excellent control over how much water is dispensed at a time.

Lastly, there's the option of an electric water pump. For this option, you will likely prefer a generator that you can run at least part-time to assist with the process, as you'll need at least 12 volts of electricity. With this choice, you do have the option to install a water heater so that you'll have continuous hot water, as well. You can also add an accumulator, which will store a little water each time the water is turned on. The accumulator will let you use a bit of water even when the power is off, which will save on noise and expense.

Then there's the toilet. Technology has come a long way in this regard, so your van won't have to be as primitive as you fear... unless, of course, you want it that way. There are a variety of road-ready commodes available that can be incorporated into your new abode with or without plumbing.

First, there are composting toilets. These toilets are chemical-free and store your waste until you can dispose of it. The secret is a peat mixture and a dehydration process. The liquids go into a separate bottle, which can be dumped securely, while the solids mix with the peat and turn into safe compost. These toilets do require power in order to work, however, as most include a small fan that keeps the process working. Composting toilets can be very expensive, but a very wise investment for those who wish to use the toilet indoors with the most minimal need for chemicals, hassle, or interacting with the resulting matter.

Then there are portable potties. These are small, self-contained toilet units that can be installed anywhere. They feature a waste tank and a water tank and can be "flushed" like a standard toilet, although what's flushed will await future disposal in the appropriate tank. This means that chemicals should be used to keep odor at bay between emptyings, though eco-friendly chemicals are also readily available. These toilets do use a considerable amount of water and can get heavy depending on how long you go between emptying.

Those traveling with children or in groups may want to invest in a full electric camper-style toilet. While impractical to install on a smaller van, this format is suitable for buses, where a waste tank can be stashed under the vehicle and dumped appropriately in waste stations at campgrounds. The benefit here is that you don't have an immediate or urgent worry about overflow, no possible spillage, and the toilet is a permanent part of your home. The downside is that it will have to be incorporated and installed, thus taking up valuable space and requiring a sizable investment.

There are also a variety of low-tech options. From what amounts to a stool with no seat, to a bucket with a seat on it, many Van Lifers have made the most of an awkward situation with a practical — if not at all glamorous — solution. There are multiple small battery-operated or hand-pump style toilets on the market as well, but bear in mind, these are often very low to the ground and still require regular and frequent emptying. Also, consider the fact that you may need to use this device at any hour of the day, in all kinds of weather. Make sure you choose a toilet option that you'll feel comfortable with at midnight during a thunderstorm!

It is possible to live without any plumbing whatsoever, of course. Water can be found in many places, and it's very simple to stock up on gallons of usable drinking water. This will, however, require room for storage. A cooler is a multi-level solution when it comes to water usage, as well. The ice used to keep food fresh in a cooler will, over time, melt. While you might not want to use that water for drinking, you can heat it up with your propane burner and a pot, and enjoy a bath or shower. You can also use that melted ice water to cool off when temperatures are climbing. Toilets can be found at gas stations, restaurants, grocery stores, campgrounds, parks, and rest areas.

When disposing of greywater and waste, it is crucial that you do not contaminate any water sources. Make sure you only dump wastewater in approved and appropriate areas. Composting toilets are less dodgy since the waste has been decontaminated naturally, but some toilet solutions include chemicals that can poison humans and wildlife, and destroy native plants and soil. Whenever possible, use biodegradable, environmentally friendly soaps, cleaners, and toilet papers.

If you choose to go the "natural" route, remember to be courteous. Step away from main areas — even if you're camping on free land, you can still avoid areas where people are likely to walk. Dig your waste trench at least six inches deep, and be sure to bury everything thoroughly once you're done.

Chapter 5: The Search Process

Once you've got all of your plans in hand, it's time to make them so. You know what size vehicle you need and likely have a top-three selection of the type of vehicle you'd like to purchase. You are confident about what you want to put in your van or bus, where it's going to go, and what you need to do to make it happen.

Now stack all of those plans neatly, and throw everything on the floor except your budget.

Shopping for your van or bus or camper can be agonizing if you have very specific requirements. You may choose to wait until you are able to locate The Exact Perfect Vehicle for your adventure. Alternatively, you may choose something that is more of a compromise on your exact requests but meets all your requirements. The choice is entirely your own.

The internet is a fantastic place to find Van Life resources. As a community that has no physical footprint (or rather, one that is always in motion), there are many forums and sites where van dwellers meet up to share thoughts, ideas, and ask each other questions. In fact, we've included some of these in the **resource section** of this book.

As you read through these forums, you'll find discussions about particular types of vans or skoolies, as well as sales ads. Some people within the van community make a fair living off rehabbing and selling vehicles. Others find that they "outgrow" their van and are ready to step up to a bigger, more off-road capable, or in some cases, more frugal vehicle.

Another online resource is vehicle sales sites. Again, we've compiled a few suggestions to get you started in the **resource section**. There are sites dedicated to vans and buses, but you can also find some good deals on regular automotive sites, especially if you're looking for a cargo or conversion van that you can take down to the bare floor and remodel into your own.

There is some debate as to whether it's worth it to reach out to regular car dealerships. The answer is yes. Shopping for a van is not unlike shopping for any other specialty item, like antique glass or rare book printings. You never know where they're going to turn up. You might find just the right base vehicle has come into a dealership as a trade-in and swipe it up before they list it on an online auction. One benefit to this plan is that dealers seldom let vehicles leave their lot without at least a full inspection. Though they might not take the time, or invest the money into fixing anything that's out of sorts, they'll at least be aware and disclose this information to you. Auctions are another great resource, if you're ok with buying vehicles "as is." You might not know its issues, problems, or need for repairs until you get it home and start truly inspecting it, but the vehicle you purchase at an auction can be extremely cheap.

Online auctions have similar perils — you are relying on the word of the person selling the vehicle, and you may not be able to physically inspect the vehicle until you have already paid for it. Still, online auction sites can bring great luck to those who have done their homework and are ready for just about anything.

If you're specifically looking for a bus, you can reach out directly to the source for more information about obtaining one of their decommissioned vehicles. For skoolies, you can reach out to the school district. Frequently, their vehicles pass through local auto auctions, but it's possible the school district might be interested in making a deal, for the right price.

When it comes to coach-type buses, you might need to do a bit more digging. National bus lines will have a point of contact for decommissioned buses, but if you're dealing with a more local outfit, it might require a few calls and emails before you find the right person.

The city transit department will likely have information about what happens to city buses once they're removed from duty. In many cases, they end up in junkyards, auctions, or are donated to various programs, but again, you might be able to make arrangements for purchase first.

When it comes to pulling the trigger and purchasing your vehicle, you must feel fully confident in your decision. You must have addressed all budget considerations, all repair requirements, and be ready to shoulder the burden of any rehab and remodeling that will be needed to make your van or bus your new home.
We encourage everyone to do as much research as possible. Find a

handful of options. Decide what things you can compromise on and what features are absolute necessities. Can you wiggle on price? What if you find a vehicle that has higher mileage than you'd like, but the price is perfect, and it's been well-cared for? It is highly unlikely that you'll find a vehicle that meets all of your needs precisely. What is far more likely is that you'll find a vehicle that shows you what features, options, and qualities are really most important to you.

If it is at all possible, try to test drive the vehicle. This might mean doing some traveling. Worse yet — this might mean getting your hopes up, traveling, and discovering it's not going to work.

You will have to feel comfortable driving your new home. In the case of a larger bus, it will take time before driving such a massive vehicle feels natural, but if a simple trip around the block feels desperately uncomfortable for any reason, it might be a good time to head back to the drawing board. There are things that can be altered, improved, or modified, but if you decide you really don't like the way driving a van with a manual transmission feels, it might be less expensive to check out options with an automatic transmission, rather than replace the entire system.

You'll also want the opportunity to really inspect the vehicle in detail. This means you might have to take a crash course in the year, make, and model of the vehicle you're going to check out, but it's better to be fully informed than guessing.

Additionally, see what maintenance and repair records you can get your hands on. The more you know about this particular vehicle's history, the more you can plan for future issues — or at least identify what needs your immediate attention.

Advice from the Road– Part 2

When it came to purchasing our first van, I was adamant that it would have a kitchenette, or at least a purposed food-prep area with storage and running water. My plans for the interior included a fold-out table, which I could use as a work station during the day, and could do extra duty as an eating surface, a drying rack for dishes and laundry, or a spot where we could hang out and play games or plan the next leg of our voyage.

I wanted an automatic transmission. I wanted a vehicle no more than 25 years old. I was fine with higher mileage, as long as it was well-cared for and didn't come with any major problems. I didn't care about color, and I wasn't fussy about how the sleeping area was set up.

We ended up with a VW Vanagon from the 1980s. It did not have a kitchen area. It didn't have a fold-out table. It didn't have so much as a shelf. In the back was a platform and a mattress... that's it.

Instead, it had a recently replaced engine. It had been regularly serviced for the past 30 years. It had only had two owners and still had its original owner's manual (which is roughly the same size as a 1980s phone book, by the way). It came with a automatic transmission, as he hoped, and a gaudy peace sign sticker... which actually hid a deep ding in the side of the door.

Was it the van I had planned on purchasing? Absolutely not. Was I completely wooed by its mechanical soundness, ease of operation, and blank-slate space? Very much so.

We looked at several dozen vans. Some of them we just courted online until the inevitable Huge Issue came to light. We had the chance to kick some of the tires. But when we found this van, two states away, in a heated, climate-controlled garage, I knew that this was the main contender for our future home on wheels.

Section 3: Creating and Maintaining a Budget While on the Road

There are so many factors that go into both creating and maintaining a budget while you're on the road. Here we'll attempt to walk through the process in easy-to-handle pieces.

If you've even started considering your Van Life budget, your head is probably a whirlwind of figures, with questions like:

1. What can I afford to spend each month?
2. What splurges or luxury items will I allow myself?
3. What happens if I run out of money?
4. If I buy this item now, will it cost me more or less in the long run?
5. What'll I do in an emergency? (Followed by feelings of desperation and panic, usually.)

First, take a deep breath. Having an emergency while on the road is really no different than having an emergency at any other time of your life. You can't completely prepare for everything, and while it's going to be deeply inconvenient, you'll have to take everything step by step to move in the right direction.

As for the rest of the questions, we'll address them one by one. While we can't actually sit down with you and do the math for your particular situation, we can bring you some key points and advice from folks who have been on the road, to help you decide where to spend money, where to save money, and where to make money.

Advice from the Road: Part 3

When we first took our van out, we had nothing. Ok, that's not entirely true. We had a bed, tons of really intuitive storage, a large ice-vault type cooler with a valve on the side to empty out the water, and a propane burner with two fuel tanks. Our van didn't even have interior lights until we removed the non-functioning air conditioning unit and accidentally reconnected something.

We thought this was the best way to save money — live as basically and frugally as possible, right? Barebones means no waste, little investment, and a smaller budget. Well, it turns out that we accidentally sabotaged ourselves with this mindset.

We stocked up on what we considered "van food" beforehand. As experienced campers and hikers, we assumed we'd want to eat the same sort of thing in the van that we ate while camping. We thought we were brilliant.

Well, it turns out that, when you're parked in a camp park full of families grilling huge, juicy steaks, that dehydrated chicken curry packet doesn't look so appetizing anymore. Even worse, because your home has wheels, and because you can get an internet signal nearly anywhere, it is very, very tempting to find yourself at the local famous restaurant every night. Which would you prefer: a powdered camping meal or authentic mole enchiladas served by a woman who has her family's 300-year-old recipe?

It's easy to make excuses, too. After all, you're on the road to experience the world as it is, and that includes the local flavor — literally. Problem is, eating at restaurants eats your budget right up!

So, you learn to compromise. Head to local markets and grocery stores, and stock up on local products there. We could buy all the flavors we couldn't find at home and take them with us wherever we went.

We did have to change the cooler setup, though. We thought we were being budget-conscious by getting the less expensive cooler. Unfortunately, we ended up wasting a lot of food when it got "drowned" in the melting ice.

As a result, we had to modify our entire setup. Just for food? No — to make the most out of our budget. Our no-power, no-water setup was tweaked into a solution that actually reduced our spending. We use only three 160-watt solar panels, which connect to four batteries. These also keep us working while we're on the road. We no longer have to stop at cafes or restaurants and buy something for the privilege of "borrowing" electricity and WiFi — we're self-reliant. (Think about it — even if you just buy a $3 snack each day for an hour of guilt-free power, that's $90 a month, and that's with a very low estimate!)

Even better, we have far less food waste. We invested in a more expensive cooler, which plugs into the van's cigarette lighter socket while we're on the road and can connect with the solar battery converter when we're not in motion. Just in case, we have several cooler packs that don't leak, spill, or otherwise ruin our food. We also have a full series of BPA-free food storage containers of all sizes, so if we do need to temporarily run on ice, we lose nothing.

Do we still try out local cuisine at restaurants? Sure, from time to time. But choosing to be able to store and prepare our own fresh food is a decision that required a little more spending on the front end but has saved us literally thousands of dollars each month!

Chapter 1: Determining Your Budget

At its core, a budget is simply a balance between money you have and money you need (or want) to spend. When you live in a fixed, permanent location, it's pretty easy to see what you have, what you need, and what to expect from month to month. After all, our daily routines rarely change overall — and that's why the road is calling to you!

Still, there's something to be said for predictability. Most of us rest easier with at least some perceived control over our daily, weekly, and monthly expenses.

It may feel, at first, like heading out on the road is going to be a complete upheaval of your way of life. In many ways, this is true. But there are plenty of things that aren't going to change about your lifestyle. You'll still need to eat every day. You'll still need to drink plenty of water. You'll still have dirty laundry.

We've included a chart that includes some common ongoing expenses. Bear in mind that this chart only includes expenses that you'll encounter on a continuous basis—we'll get to the start up and packing expenses in a moment.

This is, of course, just a guide to get you started. If you have children on the trip, some of these categories might change a bit. The maintenance for any equipment you install, such as toilets, generators, hot water heaters, and such, will be dependent on what type of equipment you choose and its specific requirements. If you have a pet, you'll need to take their needs into consideration. However, this chart should get you started in the process of thinking about what you need on a running basis.

Expense Category	Considerations	Your Calculation
Fuel	Price per Gallon Miles per Gallon Distance Traveled Fuel Cost Fluctuations (by location) Emergency Fuel Supply	
Maintenance	Oil changes (5-10,000 miles) Tire rotation (5-7,000 miles) Air filter Fluids (Radiator, Transmission, Coolant, Brake, Air Conditioning, Washer, Power Steering) Glass Cracks Windshield Wiper Blades	
Location	Parking pass Camping pass Park entry fees Showers Hotels (if necessary) Greywater dump fees (charged at some campsites)	
Kitchen Supplies	Drinking water Food/Groceries Cleaning tools	

Health	Toiletries (shampoo, toothpaste, soap, etc.) Vitamins Medications (both prescription and OTC) First Aid supplies (bandages, antiseptic cream, cotton swabs) Sunscreen Bug spray Regular medical check-ups, vaccines, dental care	
Laundry	Detergent Laundromat costs	
Entertainment	Entry fees Park passes Restaurants Cafes/Wineries/Breweries/ Distilleries/etc. Gifts/games/toys	
Other ongoing expenses	Insurance (Medical, Vehicle, etc.) Generator upkeep (if used) Vet bills (if you bring a pet) Credit card bills Van payment (if you take out a loan for the van) Roadside Assistance Program Cell phone bill WiFi	
Expenses from Home (applies only if you choose to maintain your home while you're on the road)	Mortgage/rent Electric/gas/water House sitter/tenant Insurance Taxes	

When you're filling out these expenses, try to be both practical and generous in your estimates. No matter where you're traveling, the cost of living is largely based on location. A gallon of water that costs 60 cents at one grocery store might cost $1.09 at another store twenty miles away. You can shop around for bargains, but that might cut into your fuel budget. Unless you're able to really sit down and cruise the internet to find deals at local stores and any relevant coupons, try to plan things out.

You might notice that we included "expenses from home." For some van dwellers, it's impossible to break a lease or sell property in time to get on the road. Some actually maintain their homes, so they have a "base" to return to from time to time. They might have a tenant renting the home or sublease an apartment. If you choose to maintain a stationary home, there will be expenses associated with that location — a mortgage in your name, bills, etc. You'll definitely not want any unpleasant financial surprises while you're on the road, so be sure that you factor in those regular payments if you will have them.

There are also things you can stock up on beforehand, to some extent and expenses that you will only encounter at the start of your trip, and perhaps rarely afterward. Let's take a look at what those might look like.

Expense Category	Considerations	Your Calculation
Emergency Supplies	Storage bin Tarps Bungee cords Duct tape Road flares Jumper cables Tire patch kit Spare gas canister Jack Tool kit	
Camping/Outdoor Supplies	Storage bin Tent/equipment Backpacks Sleeping bags Flashlights/lanterns Batteries Multi-tool	
Health and Wellness	Mirror Tote for toiletries Scissors Towels Storage for dirty laundry	
Bedding	Pillows Sheets Variety of blankets Mattress/sleeping surface Storage for unused bedding	

Kitchen	Large container to store canned/boxed/dry food Cooler or refrigerator Small containers for open food/leftovers Pots and pans Cooking tools (spatula, serving spoons, can opener, bottle opener) Eating utensils Dishes Burner or stovetop Fuel for cooktop Dish bin Dishrags	

Again, this is not a comprehensive list for every possible scenario, but a few helpful guidelines to get you thinking about what items are part of your necessary routine.

Many of these items will need to be replaced depending on the length of your trip, and in case there is any accidental damage. Overall these will not be things that need to be replaced weekly or even monthly.

Advice from the Road: Part 4
A word about storage.

Everything in your van will need a place to live. Everything.

One of the most challenging parts of living in a van is the fact that you can't put your dirty laundry on a chair and deal with it on laundry day. You can't just let the dishes hang out overnight in the sink. Your van will become very crowded, messy, stinky, and full of pests unless you stash your dirty laundry somewhere, keep your dishes clean and put away, and your surfaces tidy.

Worse yet, if you leave food sitting out, you run the risk of attracting bears, coyote, wolves, and more. While not naturally aggressive, these critters are very interested in any tasty tidbits you might have onboard, and they're naturally equipped with the claws and jaws that will help them get what they want!

When we hit the road, we started with several large bins:

- One for our emergency supplies, which we labeled the Oh S**t Kit
- One for the kitchen goods, which included dry foods and all of our kitchenwares
- One for our camping gear, so if it got wet or muddy, it wouldn't roll all over the van and make a mess
- One for our dirty laundry — trust me, you want something that seals, especially if you're going to be hiking ten miles a day!

These were each 60 gallon "under the bed box"-style heavy duty bins with lockable lids, specifically chosen to fit under the sleeping area. We could reach under the bed at any time and slide out the bin we needed — which we could identify because they were labeled on all four sides. The labels weren't anything fancy; just a strip of duct tape with the "Kitchen," "Camp," and so on written in permanent marker.

Under the shelf where these large bins lived was a storage area accessed by smaller doors. This had been where the original owner stored his emergency kit. We chose to create 6-quart sized plastic bins with lids to place in this area. They fit perfectly through the small door, and that way, wouldn't roll around or require additional containment.

We each had two — I chose to make one my toiletry kit — I put my shampoo, conditioner, soap, toothpaste, toothbrush, and hairbrush in one bin. That way, whenever we stopped at a place that had showers or ran into a rest stop to brush our teeth and wash our faces, I didn't have to pick and juggle what I needed — just grab the box and go. And since it had a lid, I didn't have to worry about things falling out and getting lost. If you've ever had a toothbrush fall on a rest area floor, you know that sinking feeling in your stomach when you lose an important piece of equipment!

My second bin held what I considered my daily necessities: medication, a spare phone charger, hair ties, the muscle rub I put on at night, dry shampoo, hand lotion, lip balm, sunburn cream, and my mobile TENS unit. I also had a small bottle of air freshener in there, for that "we really need to make today laundry day" vibe.

When it comes to living in a van, space is at a premium. You don't want things rolling around while you're driving, and you don't want to search all over the place when you're looking for something. If you can create a storage solution for every major area of your daily life, you'll make life so much easier for yourself.

You just have to remember to put everything back where you found it!

Chapter 2: Sticking to It

Now that you have an idea of what your expenses are going to look like, you've got to put some guidelines in place to help you stick to this plan. You know yourself best of all, so if you feel like there will be some moments of excess — such as visiting your favorite theme park or splurging at a restaurant you've always wanted to visit — make sure you add these into your budget at the outset. Just like when you lived in a stationary home, you want to make sure you have as much control over your money as possible.

There are many things you can do to keep your budget low, but you'll have to do some research and planning to carry out these options.

For example, making your own food is going to be considerably less expensive than eating at restaurants several times a week. But, as mentioned in Advice from the Road: Part 3, you'll need to be adequately prepared. Living on ramen every night is neither enjoyable nor nutritious. Make sure you incorporate methods for storing canned, boxed, and dry food, as well as produce, proteins, juices, leftovers, and other things that need to be kept chilled. This way, you'll be able to create healthful, tempting, budget-friendly meals without wasting food. We'll provide some tips on this topic in a later chapter.

Another place where you can save loads of money is by scouting out free parking and camping. Your online van community is possibly the best resource for finding a free place to catch some rest with travelers sharing some of their favorite spots for anyone who is currently on the road.

While there is nothing wrong with pulling into a paid campsite for the night, it can start to eat away at your budget. Many campsites require a $20-$40 per night camping fee, and if they have any extra perks, like vault toilets, WiFi, electricity, water hookups, laundry, or showers, there might be an additional fee to use those services.

Whenever possible, consider finding free camping. In the United States, National forests and wildlife areas and land owned by the Bureau of Land Management, they welcome free camping — as long as the land isn't privately owned. You'll need to do your homework in order to discover these spots, however, and there are several areas where there simply aren't public lands. We've included a few links in the **resource section** to guide your search.

Staying Green is another way to keep expenses down. This includes things like choosing reusable rags over paper products. Using as little water as possible for cleaning and reusing your greywater in practical ways or other options. If you use a generator, consider running it as little as possible. Try solar-powered flashlights — they can charge in the sunshine on your dashboard during the day and light up the van at night. If you don't need to be in motion, stay parked.

Anything you can do yourself saves you an expense, too. This includes maintenance and repair of nearly everything that's in your van or skoolie. If you can learn to perform minor mechanical repairs, you'll only need to pay for parts. If you can repair your own clothing, you won't need to replace it. If you have a roof rack and a sunny day, perhaps you save your quarters on a dryer and air dry your laundry.

Lastly, it's not a bad idea to sign up for fuel perks or discount programs, especially at national chains. Fuel is going to be a constant expense, and if you have the ability to earn discounts, you'll certainly be able to take advantage of them. You might also choose a credit card program through a gas station that provides discounts on fuels and products purchased from that chain. You may also stock up on gift cards for particular gas stations — some of them offer heavy discounts if you purchase gift cards in bulk. Investigate all of your opportunities to save on fuel, since you'll have absolutely no way of predicting what a gallon of gas will cost from one day to another!

Chapter 3: Earning Income While on the Move

If Van Life is to become your full-time lifestyle, you'll need either a very large amount of money before you hit the road, or you'll need regular income. More and more van dwellers are choosing to work while they're on the move. This can take on many shapes.

1. After completely rehabbing and rebuilding a van, you might find you're rather handy. Whenever money runs low, you go into a town, advertise as doing handy jobs, and make a few bucks.

2. You keep going until your funds drop below a certain limit. At that point, you pull into a semi-permanent camp park and get a job in town for a few months. You continue to live in your van, but you show up at the worksite, put in your hours, and let the income accumulate until you reach a comfortable spot where you can pick up and start driving again.

3. You keep your current job and work from the road. Many corporate-type jobs are allowing employees to telecommute from home or other alternative work environments. Your employer might require you to be signed on or otherwise reachable by phone and email during certain times of certain days, so you'll

need to plan wisely to have a reliable WiFi and phone signal during those times.

4.   Freelancing is another career path that is gaining in popularity. Again, you'll need a fairly continuous WiFi signal and phone connection, but if you have a talent, you might check popular contracting sites for jobs you can accomplish anywhere you choose to be.

5.   The Internet. We live in an age where you can get paid for talking about yourself on the internet. If you're a talented writer, photographer, videographer, or have the gift of gab, you can consider blogging, a YouTube channel, or a podcast. You'll have the ability to charge for ad space and make money by posting sponsored ads.

There are, of course, other types of income opportunities, but the main purpose of these examples is to help you appreciate that you don't have to be a trust fund baby or have millions in the bank before you hit the road.

Depending on the lifestyle you hope to lead, the compromises you're willing to make, and the skills you're willing to learn, anyone can hit the road at any time. It's just a matter of making sure you're very prepared for all of the possibilities and realities.

Advice from the Road: Part 5

I actually started my freelancing career from the road. Because I didn't want to spend the time and effort of sending all of my friends and family post-cards, I started a blog. As I was blogging, my friends would read about my adventures and share the link with their friends, and so on.

After a while, I started getting contacted by people who liked my writing style. They would have little writing projects they needed help with, and would I mind helping them out for a few bucks? Soon, I was devoting about an hour a day to these road projects.

I didn't plan to make money while on the road, but WiFi, Google Docs, PayPal, and the like make it super easy to gain a few bucks here and there. It wasn't long before I realized this was a real passion of mine, too!

Section 4: Preparing for Your Trip

We've discussed some of the preparations in earlier sections, but this one is designed to help you get really road ready. From this section you'll be able to not only make a checklist of things to pack but have places to pack them, and an orderly system for loading and unloading everything you've got. Furthermore, when things go sideways, you'll be prepared with alternatives!

Chapter 1: Your Utilities

When you were building or buying your van or skoolie, you made some very important decisions about things like power, water, toilets, showers, and more. Here is where you make sure you're ready to hit the road with all of these things!

For your power supply, both generators and solar power have special considerations. Do you have all of the knowledge and necessities to keep your generator in good, functioning order? What is your plan for running your generator? What happens if your generator goes out? You should always have a backup plan, such as flashlights and meals that don't require heating (or a heating source that doesn't require power). Does your toilet run off the generator? That's another possibility you'll need to consider.

Where are you going to get your water? Where are you going to dispose of your greywater? What if you run out of water? What are you going to store your water in? What happens if that storage tank gets damaged?

Much like you probably have a plan at home for what to do if the power goes out or a sewer main breaks, you'll need similar alternatives when you're on the road. At the same time, your storage space will be at a premium, so whatever you choose must be as simple as possible. If you are traveling with a family, for example, perhaps the path of least resistance is checking into a hotel for the night while you repair and re-sort all of the equipment that needs attention. If you're on your own, perhaps you stay put for the night, pitch a tent, and make the most of the situation.

Chapter 2: Sleeping Arrangements

When you were building your van or buying your van, you designated space for sleeping. Now that you've built your nest, it's time to feather it!

Your bed is actually a very important part of the van life experience. After all, if you sleep poorly, you might experience unnecessary back and neck pain, or become tired more easily, or just feel generally foggy and groggy. None of these are helpful when you are supposed to be driving or having adventures.

At the same time, it's generally not practical to have a king-sized thermal adjustable massaging bed installed in your van! Thankfully, there are plenty of options on the market when it comes to creating a sleeping environment that will be comfortable for you.

Start with a solid, flat, even base. Then add a mattress layer. Because you're working in a van, you might not be able to just wander into a mattress store and grab a standard commercial mattress. Instead, you might have to do some tailoring.

Futon mattresses tend to be a great medium for the base of your mattress layer. They're designed to be rolled up or folded, so if you need to stash your bedding while you drive, a futon mattress will not be offended. They're also typically stuffed with foam or padding. This means that if you cut into one to make it the right size, you can always just adjust the dimensions of the stuffing and sew it back up. Yes, this will require a little sewing skill, but it doesn't necessarily have to be gorgeous — just rugged and functional.

One thing to keep in mind with this type of mattress is that it isn't necessarily intended to be slept on every night for long periods of time. Do your research as you shop to find one that will be durable, and take care to flip and rotate your mattress often to ensure it wears evenly.

Another option is an inflatable mattress. If you need to use your sleeping area for other functions during the day, an inflatable mattress can be deflated and stashed in a relatively small area. The only downsides to this is that you will need to re-inflate it every time you use it, and it is possible for an air mattress to get tiny rips and holes that will need to be repaired in order for you to continue using it. Furthermore, you'll need to make sure the mattress fits within the dimensions of your sleeping area. Still, there are some very sturdy and comfortable air mattresses available.

On top of the mattress layer, you can add a variety of orthopedic and temperature regulating pads, which are available at most department stores and discount stores. A simple "egg-crate"-style pad might do the job, or you might want to find something that's more sturdy, firm, and will balance out your mattress. Make sure the padding you choose can be sized to your mattress, and if you're going to roll it up and store it when it's not in use, make sure it doesn't create too much unnecessary bulk. Some of the padding on the market might be as thick (or thicker!) than your mattress which could cause storage issues.

You might also consider getting what is affectionately termed a "bug bag" if you choose a non-inflatable mattress, especially if you plan to spend a lot of time in the true wilderness. This is a waterproof, insect-proof, crumb-proof mattress cover, which typically zips to keep the mattress truly protected from all of the elements. This might seem like an unnecessary extravagance until you knock over your water bottle onto your bed in the dark or find a swarm of ants casually enjoying a crumb of food you didn't realize you dropped. If you tailor your mattress to fit the space, it might not be a perfect fit, so buy a size bigger than whatever your mattress started as. You can always use bands or clips to keep it from rustling around as you sleep. Additionally, you'll be able to store your rolled-up mattress and pad in this if necessary.

Next comes the bed sheets and linens. Go with what makes you comfortable, but doesn't require a ridiculous amount of storage. You might see glorious social media pictures of van beds stacked with throw pillows. If you need throw pillows to be physically or mentally comfortable — get them. For the most part, however, you'll need enough pillows to keep your body comfortable, a fitted sheet to keep everything together, and some assortment of blankets for your preferred sleeping temperature.

Keep in mind that temperature can be a hard thing to regulate in a van, especially if you will not have a power source. You may choose to use your sleeping bag in colder climates, or if you're going to be in hotter locations, a light sheet or nothing at all. If you enjoy sleeping with a comforter in a climate-controlled house with a fan blasting directly at you, your sleeping situation might change once you're on the road.

This is another scenario where doing a test run in your garage, basement, or corner of a room will be a good idea. Set up your mattress, pad, and all the accessories you'd like to try. See how it feels, and adjust as necessary. This way, when you finally get out on the road, you'll be in a comfortable, familiar bed.

Remember also that your sheets and blankets will have to hang out in your van. Eventually, they will need to be washed and changed. You might want to have a spare set of sheets on hand and put the used sheets in with the dirty laundry. The goal is to be minimalist, but you need to be practical, as well. If you're the type of person who can wash and dry their sheets as necessary, then you'll be able to get away with just one set.

If you do choose to bring extra bedding, make sure you store it in a sealed container or bag. If you plan on going on any outdoor adventures, you will find that mud, sand, dirt, rocks, and snow will get everywhere. Make sure your clean linen stays clean until you're ready to use it by keeping it stowed away.

Another thing to consider when it comes to sleeping and bedding is windows. Yes, windows.

If you have a skoolie, you may have a lot of windows. That can be a huge advantage because you can open them at night and let the soft night air cool you while you sleep. In addition to the night air, however, you'll also let in the insects, pollen, falling leaves and seed pods, small intelligent rodents, and any looky-loos who might want to peep the interior of your home. All of these are incredibly irritating.

For windows that you'd like to keep open, you'll want to consider screens. You might have to make these yourself. Buy the kits for this at hardware stores. The best part is they don't take much work. You'll have to decide if you want to permanently install the screens or fashion them so they can be popped in when the windows are open. The second option is going to be most convenient, but less secure. A particularly clever rodent or curious person could figure out how to pop them right back out.

What about privacy windows? If you're living in a van, it's highly likely that you have a large rear window. Tinting it for privacy is possible, but be warned that different states have different laws on how dark windows can be. Instead, you might wish to fashion a privacy curtain that can be pulled across the window at night. You can install an actual curtain or use Velcro strips adhered around the van window to hang a blanket or other fabric across the window.

When thinking about window covering, remember that anything you have in the van will get dusty and dirty (maybe even smelly!). The insides of your windows will also gather condensation from your breath as you sleep on cool nights, so make sure your window treatments aren't going to be spoiled by getting slightly damp.

Your main goals for creating your sleep setting will be comfort, climate, the ability to stow and set up quickly and easily, cleanliness, and a sense of privacy. Together, these elements can't necessarily guarantee you a perfect night of sleep, but they'll certainly help!

Advice from the Road: Part 6

The first night in our van, I imagined that everyone was looking in on me. I tried to hide with the blankets over my head, but it was so hot. Eventually, I started feeling more and more comfortable with leaving the windows cracked, and then fully open.

That's when the mosquitos came out. Great big, blood-sucking mosquitos. The van was absolutely filled with them, buzzing all night, feasting on our faces. Even in the mountains, where there was snow, they still came to visit.

We quickly put up makeshift screens in the windows, but it wasn't long before the bugs found all the holes. Our next investment was perfectly-sized screens, which we affixed to the window frame with large, industrial-strength Velcro strips. The screens stowed neatly behind the driver's seat, and extra Velcro is an easy investment.

The result was a quiet night of sleep with peaceful mountain breezes and no bug attacks!

Chapter 3: Storage Solutions

Much like power sources, storage solutions are something we've touched on several times already. As you prepare to hit the road, it's crucial to really get everything organized and accounted for.

As you pack, you'll find that there might be a few things that you don't quite have a spot for. This happens to every single person as they pack up for their maiden voyage. It is highly likely that you will overpack due to "The Unknown," which will leave you scrambling for space.

Many of us pack like we're fleeing quickly, but the good news about gearing up for your new life in a van is that you have time to be strategic and plan what you pack.

Clothing

When it comes to clothing, you're probably thinking you'll need a few day-time outfits, something comfortable to wear while driving, stuff to hike and do other outdoor activities in, and probably something civilized to wear if you decide to go out to a restaurant, museum, or other "citified" location.

It's important to note, that most clothing can do a lot of work in between washings. The jeans you wear while driving might be perfectly fine for touring a local art museum. The leggings you wear while hiking through a National Park might do the trick for driving long distances the next day.

That's not to say that clothing won't get soiled or damaged and need immediate laundry or replacement, but it's unlikely that you'll need to prepare with four pairs of pants per day. Instead, plan to hand wash anything that needs immediate attention (which you can handle in your dish tub — making the most out of everything!).

If you plan to do a lot of outdoor activities, you will want to make sure you pack plenty of clean, appropriate socks and the correct footwear. You might find yourself packing more pairs of shoes than pairs of jeans, depending on what your trip has in store for you. Hiking, running, canoeing, rock climbing or caving, and water sports all require different types of footwear, as well as storage options that can contain mud, dirt, water, and odor.

Additionally, you'll need to make sure you've got climate-related gear. Fleece jackets, water-proof windbreakers, swimsuits, and even sweaters or sweatshirts might be a great thing to pack. Just remember — you don't need to bring ALL of them.

If you're the type to overpack for a vacation, start by pulling everything you want to take with you out of the drawers and closets. Then reduce that by half. Then reduce by half again. Keep paring down until you have about seven to ten days of clothing options. You might want to check out the Capsule Wardrobe method and apply this to your overall wardrobe selection. Your goal is to carry less but to have more options.

You can always wash your clothes. You can always buy something on the road if a particular need arises. But once you're on the road, the only way to get rid of things you want to keep is to pack them up and ship them to someone who will store them for you!

Supplies

And then you've got all of your supplies. This can range from your break-down kit to your pots and pans, to your toiletries, and so on.

If you've got built-in cabinetry, that's going to solve a lot of problems. At the same time, remember that your van or skoolie is going to be in motion. That means braking, accelerating, hard turns, winding roads, bumps, and potholes. The objects in your cabinets will shift and move, which can make a mess, or leave a bump on your head in the case of overhead bins.

Many van dwellers like to create storage solutions that prevent things from moving around too much while the van is in motion. One way to do this is to group items in plastic bins. Bins with lids can be especially helpful when it comes to making sure vital supplies don't escape and roll around while you're driving. There are also rack-style shelving solutions that can be installed in cabinets that help keep things stable. Velcro, magnets, bungee-style cords, tie-downs, and more are all very helpful resources in keeping things in place during transit, too.

If you do use bins, it's a good idea to keep them all labeled or color-coded for easy access. Additionally, make sure certain items can be accessed inside or outside the van. It's unlikely that you'll want to open the rear door and stand in the pouring rain to find a can opener.

Anything you can do to make the contents of your van stable and accessible will go a long way toward extending the comfort and usability of your van's contents. For the most part, this will take practice. Things that seem to make sense before you hit the road might take a different shape once you get used to the overall flow of van living.

Chapter 4: Emergency Kit

When you think of an "Emergency Kit," the first thing that probably comes to mind is a first aid kit. A first aid kit is an absolute necessity, but the emergency kit includes so much more. After all, you're preparing for unplanned events in a home that's on wheels, powered by many moving mechanical parts.

When thinking about what to put in your emergency kit, first consider the relatively common incidents that might occur to a motor vehicle. For example, flat tires. If you're driving a large transit bus, you're not going to be able to just head over to the shoulder and pop the spare on. But for smaller vans, a spare tire, jack, and tire iron are a great idea. You might even bring a tire patch kit, in the event of minor issues that can be addressed shortly at a tire shop.

What about jumper cables or a battery jump kit? Many of the older vans don't include automatic headlights or even an annoying buzz or beep to let you know you've left your lights on. You don't want to be stuck in the middle of actual nowhere, with no cell phone signal and no battery power.

A fire extinguisher is a very important addition to any emergency kit. Depending on the size of your vehicle, you might want to bring a few along, for the inside of the vehicle and for the vehicle itself. While a fire is unlikely, it is possible. And if you're planning to brave the wilderness? You might not be within easy access of emergency services.

A tarp may seem unnecessary. After all, vans and buses have roofs, and they're pretty leak proof. The issue is the windows. Glass is prone to cracks and breakage, and having water streaming through the inside of your van is no one's idea of a good time. While a tarp and duct tape aren't a permanent fix, they will help take care of the issue while you create a plan. Tarps also make a pretty handy landing pad, tent base, canopy for loung- ing outside, "spare room," and more. If you're using an outdoor hanging shower, you can use the tarp as your "floor" so you don't have to stand in mud. The uses go on and on, making a pretty convincing argument for having a tarp on hand... just in case!

Battery-operated lighting is also a good idea. This can take the form of flashlights, small lanterns, and more. Don't rely on your cell phone flashlight as a light source. If you find yourself without power and need light for a lengthy period of time, using your phone flashlight will just drain the battery. Instead, save that battery, and use a device that doesn't have the ability to call for help! Make sure you pack spare batteries as well — don't assume that you'll be able to get more whenever you need them. Batteries take up very little room and are worth it to not find yourself in a dark and scary situation.

Solar flashlights and lanterns are also fine options — just make sure you let them see the sun during the day, so they're charged when you need them.

Depending on where you're going to spend your time, you might want an emergency water purification kit on hand. While you'll largely be able to plan ahead to manage your water supply, you might find yourself in a dry location with a leak. Being able to instantly replenish your water supply is a huge benefit, no matter where you are, or what type of adventure you're having. If you're relying on a fixed freshwater tank, make sure you have a backup plan. That can even mean having a few gallons of drinking water from the grocery store on hand — just make sure you've got them stashed away in a safe location, where they can't move around and possibly spring a leak while you're driving!

Having a spare gasoline can onboard can also be helpful, especially if you're going to be traveling through long stretches of uninhabited territory. The most important consideration for having gasoline onboard is storing it properly, so it doesn't tip and spill, become too hot or too cold, or accidentally release harmful fumes into the cabin. If you have children or pets with you, you'll want to be absolutely certain they can't accidentally come in contact with the gasoline directly, either.

If you've learned some of the basics of vehicle maintenance, you'll want to have a toolset onboard also. Generally speaking, this will include a hammer or mallet, and the right-sized wrenches for all of the pieces and parts within your vehicle. You might also want a screwdriver that fits the interior screws, just in case something works loose. First-time van dwellers are always a bit surprised at what things work loose when traveling consistently over bumpy roads! There's no need to take any tools that have no use in your vehicle, so make sure you pack wisely and organize well. A small toolbox or carrying case will save you tons of frustration when you're already upset about a breakdown.

Other helpful things to have onboard are items that have plenty of practical uses. Duct tape is almost always helpful for one reason or another. From temporarily taping the soles back onto your shoes, to holding a loose cabinet door down until you can fix it, to waterproofing a baseball cap, nearly every van dweller has some zany story involving duct tape coming to the rescue in a pinch. Make sure you invest in the truly waterproof, truly sticky stuff, too.

Multi-tools, such as Leatherman or Swiss Army Knives, will prove useful in a variety of situations, as well. You'll be thrilled to have one of these in your kit when you lose the nail clippers, need to cut something to size, try to open a bottle... the list goes on and on. A pocket-sized utensil with nearly infinite uses is always welcome in a van.

Matches or a long grill-style lighter can also be helpful. If you have a propane stove or burner that you'll be using, these will be a necessity, as well as if you plan on regularly building campfires. Even if you don't plan on needing to start a fire, you might find yourself in need of a heat and light resource if you lose your power source. Camping matches are a small easy-to-store investment that could really come in handy in a pinch.

In some cases, you'll want to pack several of these items. If, for example, you're a whole family on the road, you'll probably want several flashlights, which means stocking up on more batteries. If you're going to be gone for a significant amount of time, it can't hurt to have two rolls of duct tape — one in the cabin, and one on reserve with the vehicle maintenance equipment.

Now the tricky part — where do you put all of this stuff? With the exception of items that need special storage considerations, like gasoline and water, you might choose to put everything together in a tote or cabinet that is exclusively designated for your emergency kit. However, you might want to keep some of the smaller items in an easy-to-reach spot, like the glove box, or a small in-cabin kit that can be accessed quickly. After all, it makes no sense to have a flashlight if you have to fumble around in the dark in order to find it.

When it comes to emergency supplies, there's a fine line between "too prepared" and "possible catastrophe." Just like in a stationary home, it's impossible to prepare for every eventuality. It may seem even more challenging to think of all the dangers that might befall you on the road. In order to give yourself more peace of mind, do some research before-hand on the areas where you'll be traveling. What types of perils have other van dwellers encountered? Do other travelers have recommendations for supplies to have on hand? Knowing what others have experienced in that area can help give you some perspective on your own needs so you can plan ahead.

Chapter 5: Food

The topic of food has come up several times, and for good reason — we literally cannot live without it. In our stationary worlds, we pop into the grocery store whenever we need to and load up on fresh produce, meats, cheese, eggs, frozen foods, and so on. We bring them home, organize them in our full-sized refrigerators, freezers, and cabinets, and plan to use them before the expiration date. Sometimes we don't feel like cooking, so we head out to a restaurant or order delivery, and if we order too much food, we throw that in the refrigerator and reheat it in our microwaves the next day.

It is technically still possible to do all of that in a van or bus, as long as you've got the space, power, and equipment to do so. You may not have full-sized appliances and cabinets, but you can incorporate smaller, camper-style units that do the same job. This is a very good idea if you'll be traveling with children, or if you're making van living your permanent lifestyle.

For many Van Lifers, though, there is neither room nor practical need for appliances. In reality, none of the traditional kitchen appliances are required to live. An economical use of food products, a cold storage option, and the ability to heat food and water are really all it takes to keep yourself fed on the road.

As mentioned earlier, coolers are very helpful. The type of cooler you choose does have some bearing on your food options and usage, however, An ice-chest type cooler is typically very inexpensive, and melted ice can be recycled as bathwater or used for cleaning up certain non-food items (like the floor of the van, your muddy flip-flops, etc.). The downside to this is that your cooler will fill with water as the ice melts. Unless it is replenished regularly, that means that anything in the cooler can get water-logged, and anything that gets too warm has a chance of spoiling. But, if you practice extreme discipline in the use of your ice chest, there's no reason why this can't work.

Plug-in coolers can be very helpful, too. They are generally more expensive than ice chests, but you have the luxury of never worrying about the ice/water ratio. At the same time, you've got to have the power supply to keep it going. Most units require 12 volts of power, which isn't unreasonable. If you've got an older van with no power supply, however, you might be wary of leaving it plugged in overnight, as it might drain the battery. Some coolers will have the ability to keep their contents cooled if unplugged for short periods, and some will not. Food poisoning while on the road is even more un-comfortable than it is in a house or apartment, so don't tempt the fates when it comes to food safety. Make sure your food is stored at the appropriate temperature — if your cooler can't handle it, don't take the risk.

When it comes to storing produce, you have two main goals. The first is to not have it rolling around the cabin as you drive, and the second is to not attract insects or other wildlife that might be interested in sampling your meals. Generally speaking, the cooler is a fine place to keep your fruits and veggies, even if you wouldn't technically put a particular item there at home.

As for dry foods, the goals are the same as produce, only you won't necessarily want to stash everything in the cooler. Food-safe plastic storage tubs are a very good idea for things like rice and noodles and grains, as they keep the bugs out and all of the food in one place. Canned goods and other self-storing foods(like ramen noodle packets) only need to be stored in a way that they're secure and not rolling underfoot while you're trying to drive.

Snack foods and bread products are a different consideration on the road. At home, you might roll up the bag inside the cracker box, throw a chip-clip on a bag of crispy snacks, and just keep the bread shut with a twist-tie. On the road, you've got a greater exposure to insects, and living in an open-air type environment means things will go stale and grow mold more quickly. You've also got to consider curious wildlife, as well. Make sure you can tuck your snacks and bread products somewhere safe where they won't be shared without your permission.

If you're an avid camper or outdoor fan, you probably associate foods like peanut butter, trail mix, power bars, tuna, canned stew, and ramen with living outdoors. These are certainly staples of Van Life, as well, but you can diversify your diet. The key is making sure you use everything immediately, unless you have sufficient, reliable cold storage for leftovers.

When you go to the grocery store now, you might take advantage of sales, like 3 for $10 salad kits or "fill the freezer" meat deals. Without a ton of cold storage space, that's no longer going to make sense. Instead, you'll want to purchase only what you can eat or adequately store right now.

That's not to say you can't have salad or meat but that you'll want to look at portions realistically to avoid waste.

Canned and dried food is always a go-to when it comes to living in a situation where there's not a lot of space, time, or refrigeration, but these foods are often high in sodium and preservatives. Make sure you're making wise choices for your body, health, and lifestyle. Good nutrition is key to giving you stamina and helping you maintain your health while you're on the road. Make sure you're fueling your body in a way that's appropriate for you.

When planning meals, you can always take advantage of what resources you have to create back-to-back meals that will meet the requirements of multiple food groups. For example, if you purchase one salad kit, one can of beans, a bell pepper, two tomatoes, and one large chicken breast, you can have a protein-packed chicken/bean chili for dinner with a tasty side salad, then follow it up with a big salad topped with chicken for lunch the next day. Simply cook the chicken first, then cut it into two portions — the amount you'll add to tonight's chili and the bit that you'll slice up for lunch tomorrow. Make sure you put what you're not using right away into the cooler immediately. Throw the beans, a chopped tomato, and half the bell pepper into a pot with the chicken and your favorite seasonings for a tasty "road chili." Make yourself a small salad to enjoy, too, and make sure you seal up the rest and store it in the cooler. Tomorrow, you can use the other half of the bell pepper, the second tomato, the rest of the salad kit, and the leftover chicken to have a nutritious salad.

This is just one example of how being strategic with your food and resources can help you avoid "camp food burnout." There are plenty of recipe guides for low tech and outdoor living, and we've included some links in the **resources** at the end of this book. You might feel now like having a cooler and a propane camp stove will be incredibly limiting, but the reality is that you can eat almost exactly like you do at home — you just have to scale back and be more realistic about your food use. Before you start your maiden voyage, you might want to keep track of what you cook, what you eat, how many leftovers you have, and how quickly you eat those left-overs. This will give you a little more insight about your food volume usage, so you can be more adequately prepared once you get on the road.

Section 5: Where Are You Going to Go?

Your van is fully packed. You're ready to go. You're equipped with all sorts of new and exciting knowledge.

So where do you go?

For some people, there's a very obvious destination in mind. Perhaps you've spent your life pining for a visit to a particular landmark, park, or museum. Naturally, you'll want to head there immediately. But the beauty of van living is that there are no destinations — only the amazing journey. Once you've hit your ideal spot — then what? You might be feeling a bit lost.

Other people might not have a clear destination selected. They might have a few general ideas of things they'd like to see, but they haven't really figured out where to go or how to get there.

Then there's a third party, which borrows a little from the first group and the second group. These folks have a definite list of things they want to see but look forward to connecting the dots with adventure.

There's plenty of grey area in between these three options, as well. If you're worried about feeling constricted by requiring plans, you'll be glad to know that there's really no wrong way to do your Van Life. It is your practice, your lifestyle, and we're just here to tap you on the shoulder and give you practical advice and suggestions. If you're the sort of person who needs guidance or help getting started, that's also not wrong. You're allowed to be confused and overwhelmed.

Let's take a look at a few different strategies that are popular among road warriors. If you're feeling too decisive, this might help you open your mind to more possibilities. If you're feeling too free, this can help you start to reach out and explore a few solid "x" marks to put on your map for future destinations.

The "Keep Moving" Strategy

Have you ever heard the phrase "goes as the wind blows?" There are van dwellers who truly do this. If they wake up and feel like checking out the west coast, so be it. Maybe the mountains next week. How about a forest?

Having a home on wheels really does mean you can go where you want, when you want, but remember that fuel costs are a very real thing. If you have an unlimited budget, perhaps driving in perpetual circles and constantly being on the move isn't a bad thing. For those who need to be aware of every cent they spend, perhaps a little bit of planning can help temper that possible spending.

Navigation is a necessary evil, even if you just want to wander. While getting lost can be fun, it does lose its novelty when bad things happen, and you don't know where you are. It can also wind up feeling a little unnecessary and uninspiring over time.

Ultimately, the "Keep Moving" strategy can turn up some wonderful roadside surprises that you never expected to find. These lifetime experiences can never be forced, anticipated, or replaced. There is so much beauty in this world, and having the freedom to experience all the beauty you can is something many people can't even imagine.

This method does require a bit of careful compromise between wandering and respecting your budget, as well as any needs you might have for bathing, laundry, and stocking up on supplies. There needs to be a bit of conscious planning but never so much that you feel restricted.

Long-Term Living

Other people like to have the opportunity to really experience the culture of a location, even if it's just for a temporary time period.

While you might stake a claim on a particular camping spot, either within a designated camp park or out in the wilderness, that doesn't mean you can't leave and explore. As discussed earlier, some van dwellers take along a scooter or bicycle, so they can leave the confines of the van to wander — you're only limited by how far you're willing to stray from the van in one day.

Much like wandering, there are both pros and cons to this type of adventure. You might end up spending more in camping fees, due to your long-term stay, but you'll likely save on your fuel budget. Even if you do your local exploration in your van, it's likely that you'll be staying within a 20-mile radius.

Additionally, you'll be familiar with the area and some of the local options. You'll establish a place to purchase groceries, do your laundry, and replenish supplies. You might find some local entertainment options that you'd never expect to experience. Locals are a great source of knowledge, input, and recommendations that you won't find anywhere else, so it might be worth it to hang out at the local watering hole and find out when the county fair is or what local band is playing soon.

At the same time, you might find yourself feeling just a little too cozy. You might start to think that you've given up one home and just moved somewhere else. Always remember — you have the freedom to start the engine and throw it into gear anytime you want. Just figure out the next place to go, and get those actual wheels in motion!

Connecting the Dots
One fun method of travel is to turn the whole experience into a wild game of "connect the dots." You can pick a handful of things you'd really like to do while you're on the road, then mosey from point to point.

There are no restrictions on this method. You choose your timeframe and how you get from Point A to Point B. The only limits that exist are those that you create. For example, if you want to go to a concert in a specific city on a specific day, you'll need to make sure you make appropriate travel plans. Otherwise, you have the freedom to wander, without the lack of direction. In many ways, this is the best of both worlds!

Advice from the Road: Part 7

Our trip started as a fifty-page list of things we wanted to see, categorized by state. Yes. You read that right — fifty pages. There was no possible way we were going to be able to squeeze everything in, and we knew that, but still, it seemed like a good way to start.

Our first step was to pull out a huge map of the United States, including major freeways. This map was really huge — it took up our entire dining room table.

Next, we used little dot stickers to plot out some of the places we wanted to go, state by state. We put everything on there. In some states, it looked absolutely ridiculous. In other states, it was clear that we had a concentration of interest in a specific area.

The plans started to take shape from there. We knew we had a limited timeframe for our first trip (if you can call a year "limited"), so we had to create a way to see as much as possible without being too indirect.

We made a few rules to make sure we kept with our desire to explore: First, we would limit our use of major freeways and take as many back roads as possible. Second, any time we stopped, we'd check out what was going on in a five-mile radius and see what we needed to check out before we kept moving on.

We cheated a little on both of those rules. We broke the "five-mile rule" a lot, and there were a few times when we were so tired, we decided to take the fastest route instead of the scenic route to make sure we were driving safely. Still, I have absolutely no regrets about the number of things we were able to see, do, and try, and the diversity of those experiences.

Section 6: Staying Happy on the Road

We started this book by guiding you through the Van Life mindset, to see if you're prepared for this undertaking. After all, creating an entirely new lifestyle from scratch is no small task! At this point, you've got your vehicle. It's packed. You're confidently armed with a variety of literature, including repair manuals, replacement part specs, maps, pamphlets, recipes, and so on.

You probably feel pretty well prepared for anything that could happen, and you really should feel confident with all you have accomplished up to this point. Van Life is not for the weak of heart, and preparing for life on the road is a serious rite of passage.

Still, there's really nothing that can prepare you for the feeling you'll get, sitting behind that giant steering wheel, listening to your engine complain as it climbs its first winding mountain road with you.

And there's also nothing quite like the feeling of lying awake at night, on your van mattress, wishing for the thick memory foam bed you had at home, where you can fall asleep to your favorite Netflix series without worrying about burning up the power supply, in air conditioning that you can crank when it gets hot, with a shower and a toilet that require little to no maintenance in the very next room. You might just find yourself longing for a place that doesn't kind of faintly smell like shoes and laundry all the time. That's ok! You're entirely allowed to have these feelings.

In this section, we'll focus on how to keep the motivation and feelings of well-being continue even if life is starting to feel stale. While we can't cure your melancholy, we do want you to know that this is normal and happens to absolutely everyone.

Chapter 1: Avoiding Boredom

During particularly long hauls, you will likely experience boredom. Your first reaction to recognizing this boredom may be fear. You uprooted your entire life to live on the road, only to feel the same boredom you felt at home. What is wrong with you?

The answer? Nothing. You're allowed to feel stagnant, especially when you are.

The beauty of Van Life is that you can shake it up. Celebrate that you can go anywhere. If you start feeling like "all I do is drive, and I don't even like it," then go to a National Park. Hike the trails no one hikes. Or, if you're feeling lonely, hike the trails that everyone hikes. Meet new trail buddies. Let yourself be in awe of the natural beauty that surrounds you.

If, at any time, you feel like you see the same stuff every day, you need to find some hidden gems to get you out of the rut. Hop on the internet. Go into a diner or dive bar and talk to the older locals. In your life at home, you could break out of a rut by calling your friends and doing something predictable, like meeting up for coffee or a movie or drinks. On the road, if you're feeling the monotony, you need to go meet Sue, the World's Largest Cow (or whatever is "cool and unusual" in your vicinity). Do an online search for "cool and unusual things" and a location, and you'll turn up loads of things you've never even heard about!

Find out what's going on at the local college. What bands are playing? What kind of lectures or exhibitions can you find? If nothing comes to mind, just park at the end of a street, any street, walk until you don't want to keep going, then walk back to your van. You might wonder what that will accomplish. Well, what are five things you saw during your walk that were interesting?

Keep yourself in the mindset that you have control over your exploration. Though not every place you wander will feature jaw-dropping scenery, activities that make your heart race, or experiences that open your soul, there will be plenty of things that will be new to you. Embrace these.

You'll also want to keep your mind engaged while you're on the road, with activities you can enjoy within the confines of the van. There will be bad weather days. You will probably get sick or injured. Or, you just might not feel like leaving the van on a particular day. Make sure you have plenty of stuff that will keep you engaged and entertained.

A few examples include:

- Audiobooks, music, and podcasts. You don't have to stop learning and growing, just because you're no longer a part of a wall-to-wall, brick-and-mortar society! Use this opportunity to expand your horizons. Choose audiobooks that teach you about totally new topics. Listen to performers you've only heard about from your friends. Check out podcasts that will challenge your thoughts and endear you to the human experience.
- Activity books. This may seem like it's geared to kids, but adults can gain a lot from coloring, doing logic puzzles, crosswords, sudoku, or even by trying to find Waldo! When you stare at the road for hours at a time, your mind craves something different, so put your creativity and problem-solving skills to the test with some harmless activities that won't require a lot of space or supplies.
- Blogging. Though a brief glimpse through the **resources section** may make it sound like the internet is already saturated with Van Life blogs, there's always room for your experience. You can start a blog for free and use it to share your pictures and thoughts with friends and family. You might also start a variety of social media platforms specifically for your voyage. If sharing these thoughts with the whole world isn't your style, old fashioned pen-and-paper journals are always an option.

Lastly, try to take a deep breath and remember to enjoy the moment. It is very easy for depression and anxiety to creep up on you when you're on the road, especially if you're alone. As you drive, you have lots of time to stop and reflect on negative thoughts. It's easier said than done, but don't let your mind trick you like that.

Come up with a mantra that reaffirms your abilities. You have made it this far. You have created a new lifestyle for yourself. You are doing just fine. Today is always an adventure, and you have opportunities on the road that many people will never take advantage of. Remind yourself to love what you're doing. Cherish every detail, every new experience, every little thing you've never seen before.

This is your dream, and you are making it come true.

Chapter 2: Homesickness/Loneliness

Being on the road can feel very lonely sometimes. Most of us are used to living a more sedentary lifestyle or one where we can just pick up the phone and text or call our friends. You and your buddies probably get together now and then to catch up, have dinner, watch movies, and just generally hang out. It's different when you're on the road.

You can still have friends over to your van, of course, but now you have to meet new people. You'll probably visit friends and family that you don't usually get to see while you're traveling, but all the people you see every day will be exactly where you left them.

While this concept might make you feel very sad, that's not entirely bad news. They're exactly where you left them. You can go visit them. Some people feel that, since they're devoted to Van Life now, they can't go home. It's ok to go home.

There is going to come a time when both your body and soul will long for the comforts and conveniences of home. If you have the desire to go back to the place where you started your journey, go for it! Stay with friends or family back in your hometown. Go to your regular haunts. Everyone will want to hear stories, so share them! Soon, your heart will long for the road again, and off you'll go, spiritually refreshed from your visit.

You might also try planting for a bit wherever you are on the road. Find a long-term parking solution, and let yourself have a routine for a few days. Sometimes the brain and body need a sense of regularity and stability to help you put everything into perspective.

Additionally, keep your finger on the pulse of the van community. There are plenty of meetups scheduled throughout the year, even around the world. You might start conversing with your new best friends via the forums, blogs, and social media sites dedicated to those living the Van Life. Becoming a part of a community can help you with those feelings of longing and belonging.

Advice from the Road: Part 8

The first time you miss an important family event, it will break your heart. You'll see the pictures online — maybe your whole family enjoying cake together — and you'll wish you were there. You'll be able to feel all the hugs, hear the laughter, smell the over-cooked casserole, and your heart will cry out.

The first event I missed was my niece's birthday party. It was a small shindig, and really not a big deal, but when I saw the pictures of her opening her gifts, beaming at the camera, surrounded by torn wrapping paper and the bounty of her party, I cried. I wanted to be there. But it wasn't practical to be there and here, 800 miles away in the middle of the mountains.

Sometimes, you'll feel like you've done something selfish. People will try to tell you that, too. But the reality is that we all choose the lifestyle that's best for us.

You can choose to come home for the holidays, the birthdays, the anniversaries, the bachelorette parties, and so on. But the realities of time and space mean that you can't be in two places at once. You can't summit Angel's Landing and be in Florida by dinner time.

Remember that you can make room for everything and anything that you value, but you don't have to make room for everything and anything that's suggested to you. You can always go back. You can always come back. Don't let yourself feel rushed or pushed.

One tool that I began to value from the road was phone calls. It's so easy to get away with texting conversations, but when you're on the road, hearing someone's voice can be very soothing. It's also likely that there's someone who wants to hear from you, too. When you have a fully-charged battery and service, reach out — make a call. Talk. It'll do your soul some good.

Chapter 3: Housekeeping

Housekeeping might not be the most enjoyable use of time, but it's extremely necessary. If you're the type who has a "junk drawer," a "mail folder," or "a laundry chair". You might find Van Life challenging at first.

In a van, any mess you make is proportionately larger than it would be in a house or apartment. If you leave a pair of shoes on the floor of your bedroom, you can probably maneuver around them pretty easily. If you leave your shoes on the floor of your van, you will trip over them, and you will get mad at yourself for leaving them where you could trip over them.

Living in close quarters requires a new level of hygiene, which can be especially tricky when you don't have the ability to give yourself hour-long exfoliating showers every day. Keeping the stinky things stored, as we mentioned earlier, is a great way to prevent a long-term, permanent reek, but you'll still need to wash everything regularly. That includes yourself, your laundry, your bed linens, any rugs you might have, your dishes, and your commode, just to name a few. Make sure you dispose of spoiled food immediately. If you are practicing recycling on the road, make sure your empties are rinsed.

Not only do these practices cut down on bad smells, but they also cut down on bugs and critters. Wildlife is a very real part of Van Life and can include everything from the innocuous visits of birds, squirrels, and chipmunks, to the possibly dangerous curiosity of bears. You'll definitely want to avoid the headache of an ant infestation, but there's no reason to tempt a hungry grizzly!

To avoid all of this, make sure you sweep your abode on wheels regularly. Clean up any spills immediately. Get rid of trash as frequently as you can. Do your part to keep things as clean as possible.

Not only does this practice have sanitary implications, but it can also make you feel better about your dwelling. Some people feel a sense of purpose and pride when they mow their lawn or scrub their floors in a stationary home. Doing something as simple as washing all of the mud from your latest off-road excursion can remind you that you love your new home and your new life, and you wouldn't have it any other way!

In Conclusion

Is Van Life for everyone? No. The truth is that most people won't even consider, think about, or be able to fathom the idea of living in a small, mobile space. The idea of not knowing where you're going to sleep tonight, or heating up beans over a propane burner in the dark, or going to the bathroom outside at midnight might sound like an absolute nightmare to some people.

But there is a special breed of people. There are some who hear or read phrases like this, and their hearts beat a little faster and a little harder. The ideas of "opportunities" and "unknowns" sound more welcoming than fearsome. They look at the walls around them and feel like they're being crushed by stability. These are the people who are born Van Lifers.

Are you one of them? Only you can tell for sure. If there is one thing we hope you've learned from this book, it's that you can't do Van Life the wrong way. Beyond that, building your own Van Life is a process and not one that comes quickly or easily.

Can you find "any old" van, start the engine, and take off? Sure! There are some people who are naturally adaptive. But for those of us who are taking off from what feels like a very sheltered spot, there can be lots of planning and attention to details in order to feel more secure about this huge decision.

If there's one piece of advice all van dwellers should know, it's "Don't panic when things go wrong — they just will." The first time things go topsy-turvy, it will be terrifying. There will be setbacks. You will revisit the drawing board many times. The good news is that, even when things go upside down, they tend to put themselves right sideup again, as long as you don't panic.

Remember also that this isn't a competition. Just because someone on social media does it differently, doesn't mean you've failed. If you catch a cold and spend two days in a hotel recovering, that doesn't mean you're inadequate. It means you did the best thing you could for yourself in that situation. If you choose to start the day with your favorite chain restaurant doughnut and coffee, don't feel like your experience is any less authentic than the bloggers who figure out how to make overnight oats in a tin coffee mug. Just make sure you budget for the expense and get on with your best Van Life.

In short, be sure to enjoy every step of the journey. You are doing something many people dream of, but very few people get to experience.

This is the beginning of your new life.

Section 7: Helpful Resources for Future Van Dwellers

The following links lead to online blogs, reference materials, and websites that can help you with every step of the process of converting to Van Life. The views and ideas expressed in each of these links belong solely to the person writing it, so please don't consider their inclusion an endorsement or partnership. We simply wanted to get you started on the quest for more information.

Remember, there is no "wrong" way to do Van Life. There are only ways that work better for your lifestyle and things that don't work for you. It's a very personal experience that often requires a lot of trial and error.

Still, sometimes it helps to read the experiences of those who have tried it, are doing it, or are in the same position as you are when it comes to trying something very, very different.

Feel free to check out some of these links to draw inspiration, and continue your quest for more information!

The Van Life State of Mind:
As noted, you've got to be in the right headspace to really enjoy the wild ride.

http://www.alwaystheroad.com/blog/2017/3/24/is-van-life-for-you-how-to-know-if-its-right-for-you

Parking Options, Camping Options, and Sleep Spots
Tracking down a spot where you can catch up on some rest or spend the night can be challenging, especially when you're on a tight budget. Here are some resources to help you find a safe, practical place to rest.

https://www.campendium.com/camping/vanlife/
http://thevanual.com/sleeping-and-safety/

https://www.cheaprvliving.com/stealth-city-parking/bobs-12-command-ments-for-stealth-parking-in-the-city/
https://divineontheroad.com/overnight-parking/
https://kombilife.com/van-life-free-camping/
https://www.classicvans.com/
https://www.youtube.com/watch?v=oqPiP2JYVNc
https://www.nps.gov/index.htm

Choosing a Van

If the topic of vans as a vehicle is new to you, you'll definitely want to do additional research before starting the shopping process. Here are a few sites that will help you learn more about the types of vans and buses, as well as a variety of opinions to help guide you through the pros and cons of every option out there.

https://www.curbed.com/2018/1/31/16951486/best-van-conversion-rv-camper-vanlife
https://vanclan.co/best-van-to-live-in/
https://gnomadhome.com/why-choose-conversion-van-for-vanlife/
https://gearmoose.com/van-life-best-camper-vans/
https://weretherussos.com/van-chassis-camper-van-conversion/

Classic Van Lifers

As mentioned, Classic vans have a following of their own. Here are some links to resources for people who are living the "old school" way, with vans from earlier eras. Check out their thoughts, experiences, and words of advice.

https://bearfoottheory.com/category/van-life/
https://blog.feedspot.com/van_life_blogs/
https://vanclan.co/vanlife-blogs/

Skoolies

For those who are interested in larger format on-the-road living, buses are the way to go. The conversion, rehab, remodel, and updating of these vehicles could be a book on their own, so we've included a few links to folks who have gone through the process. Their insights, advice, trials, and tribulations can be helpful as you adjust to the learning curve of a great big diesel vehicle!

https://gearjunkie.com/school-bus-rv-camper-conversion-remodel
https://www.curbed.com/2019/3/6/18246221/camper-conversion-skoolie-vanlife-tiny-house
https://www.buslifeadventure.com/index.php/blog/16-blog/198-bus-life-vs-van-life-as-seen-through-the-eyes-of-a-van-dweller

The Cost of Van Living

While we've included some details about how to calculate your van shopping budget, your remodeling budget, your road budget, your overall experience budget and more, we can't predict all of the expenses that might go into your individual experience. Check out these resources for more inspiration.

https://www.moneyunder30.com/van-living
https://www.parkedinparadise.com/van-life-cost/
https://mymoneywizard.com/living-in-a-van/
https://www.explorist.life/how-much-does-van-life-cost/
https://faroutride.com/vanlife-actual-cost/

Generating Revenue on the Road

Again, we all need to follow our own path when it comes to careers, so only try this at home if you think you can make it work with your own skills, talents, and preferences. If you're feeling hesitant about trying to make a career work on the road, here are some thoughts, ideas, and words of wisdom from those who have made it happen.
https://www.thewaywardhome.com/make-money-living-on-the-road/

http://www.alwaystheroad.com/blog/2017/9/18/the-ultimate-van-life-question-answered-how-we-make-money-on-the-road
https://projectvanlife.com/van-life-money-tips/
https://vansage.com/remote-jobs-for-van-life/
https://outboundliving.com/working-making-money/
https://vacayvans.com/how-to-make-money-working-remotely-living-vanlife/
https://wandrlymagazine.com/article/make-money-in-a-van/

On the Topic of Food

Everyone has different tastes, so we tried to round up a bunch of links that cover food storage, food preparation, and on-the-road recipes that many people can relate to. The food suggestions we mentioned within the chapter aren't inclusive of all diets and preferences, so we wanted to help get the creative cooking ideas flowing with a handful of resources.

https://www.climbonmaps.com/cold-food-storage.html
https://authenticavl.com/van-life/how-to-keep-your-food-fresh/
https://vanclan.co/vanlife-recipes/
https://mpora.com/camping/12-super-simple-meals-for-when-youre-living-in-a-van/
https://www.vancognito.com/van-life-cooking/
https://www.allrecipes.com/article/three-ways-to-conquer-camper-van-cooking-vanlife/
https://vansage.com/easy-campsite-recipes/
https://theplaidzebra.com/these-5-cheap-and-easy-meal-ideas-will-give-you-the-freedom-to-take-life-on-the-road/
https://simplyvanlife.com/non-perishable-foods-for-van-life/
https://www.parkedinparadise.com/storage-organization/
http://www.nomadswithavan.com/van-friendly-foods/
https://www.youtube.com/watch?v=1zTzaeOo8_w

HOW TO CHOOSE THE ULTIMATE SIDE-HUSTLE:

Making money and being your own boss

Kristine Hudson

SECTION 1:

GETTING READY FOR YOUR NEW GIG

Wouldn't it be grand, to have the kind of life where you could control your income almost instantaneously? Where the amount of money you make today was based on how much time and effort you had available to put into making things work?

For years, it's been drilled into our heads that the only way to get a job is to "pound the pavement." That is, to go out there, find a job that will have us, interview, and then show up at the job site when we're scheduled and do our best within that role.

But there are so many problems with this business model, especially for those of us who have many, many, many other things going on in our lives. As women, we're often pulled in a million different directions at once. We're mothers, daughters, sisters, wives, students, and partners. We've got what seems like infinite responsibilities at all times. As a result, it's difficult for us to be able to put everything down in order to show up at a job at a specific time every day.

Whether it's a standard Monday-through-Friday 9-to-5 type job, or a schedule that has you working different hours every single day, it can be hard for a busy woman to juggle work commitments with all of her other duties. If only we could step back and work a job where, as long as we meet deadlines, no one cares what hours we work! Or better yet, a job where we have the ability to control how much we do in a given week to make room for all of those more pressing, life-or-death (or at least life-or-mess) situations.

Enter the "side-hustle." If you haven't heard the term before, a side-hustle is a job or gig that is used to supplement income when getting a full time job outside of the home simply isn't possible, or when you need more income than that full time job is bringing in at the moment.

In this book, we'll examine the reasons one might decide to pursue a side-hustle, as well as tips for narrowing down what type of gigs are best for you and your lifestyle. We'll also take a look at some of the different types of side-hustles, as well as why you might or might not want to check out that type of gig. We'll also share some tips for making sure you don't jump right out of the proverbial frying pan and into the fire, and how to keep yourself on target both with your life and your side-hustle. At the end of this book, we've included some helpful resources for women who are getting started with side-hustles, to help you prepare for and maintain a stress-free work/ life balance with your new gig.

Chapter 1: Why Do You Want a Side-Hustle?

Before you actually start down the road of finding a side-hustle, it's important to make sure that you're mentally, emotionally, and physically prepared. For most of us, money is always tight. At the very least, we feel like things would be a little easier if we just had a little more money.

While this is a very good reason to look for ways to make more income, it doesn't mean that it's going to be easy. After all, a job is going to be a job, no matter what. That means you will have to put in the time and effort in order to make money. You may also need to fork out a little money in order to really get your side-hustle off the ground.

There are many situations in which a side-hustle can be helpful for nearly every woman.

For example, if you're a stay-at-home mom, a side-hustle might provide just the right level of income and stimulation during the day, while the kids are at school. With flexible hours, however, you'll be able to pick up the kids from school, drive them to all of their assorted practices and activities, make dinner, keep up on housework, and not miss a beat. Since you get to make all the rules about the time and place you work, you won't have to reschedule, carpool, or miss important games.

Perhaps you're a full-time student. You've got classes all day, and projects and papers to complete once you get home. You might have an internship or work experience project that takes up a lot of time before you graduate, but makes no money at all. Still, you need to eat and pay for class, so having a gig that doesn't require a lot of hours can help you maintain a life outside of class.

Maybe you already have a part-time or full-time job, but it's just not cutting it. The pay is too low, the hours are awful, and you're heading nowhere, fast. Alternately, perhaps you really want to work for yourself, but the risk of quitting your job to do what you love full time is too great. Try looking into that passion as a side-hustle, so you can build your clientele and references, all while maintaining the stability of your regular job.

Before you get started finding the perfect side-hustle, sit down and really consider the pros and cons of wanting to invest your time, energy, and money into yet another project.

The benefits of a side-hustle are many. Once you've hit your stride, you will make more money. In many cases, you will be able to work from home, or from a location of your choosing. This makes side-hustles easier to integrate into things like your own educational studies, a day job, raising children, driving the kids back and forth from school and activities, and more.

Many mothers lament that they spend more on child care than they bring home in their paychecks. Having a lucrative side-hustle can mean earning a paycheck without having to pay for child care. If you're a student, you've probably had many stellar interviews, only to be told the employer can't work with your erratic class schedule. Unless you're available all day, every day, finding a source of income can be incredibly difficult.

If you are working a full-time job right now, you most likely have to either sacrifice a full block of eight hours to your job, or else memorize a complicated schedule that might change every week. By choosing a side-hustle, you can make sure the hours you work coincide with the time that is actually available for your use.

Finding the perfect side-hustle can also be a great benefit for those who are looking to pursue a serious dream or passion, but need to make sure they can earn enough income to live off of while they work on that dream. For example, if you've recently gone back to school to pursue a degree in your ultimate career field, it's only natural that your studies and schoolwork should be your number one priority. At the same time, you need to eat, get to class, and purchase those expensive textbooks. Having a side-hustle that you can dedicate a few hours to in between class or study breaks can be very helpful, allowing you to both follow your dreams while earning a little money to keep you afloat.

A side-hustle is also the perfect compliment to a job that's just not keeping you mentally stimulated or providing enough income. While the last thing you may want to do when you get home from work is do more work, a side-hustle can take the form of a craft or service you love to perform, such as knitting, painting, or building something wonderful with your own two hands. These activities can be incredibly stress-relieving activities for you, yet a pretty decent way to make money, as well.

The ultimate goal of a side-hustle is to bring you money, without requiring you to sacrifice the top priorities in your life. Before you get started, consider the following questions:

- How much time per day or week can I dedicate to this?
- How will I be available to communicate with clients/organizers?
- Do I truly have the capacity to take on anything else in my life right now?
- What will happen if I DON'T find a side-hustle?

The answers to these questions will help you determine if you're truly ready to pick up a side-hustle. It may be that you're very eager to make money right this very second, and sometimes that desperation leads us to biting off more than we can chew. While side-hustles are far more flexible than full time jobs, they will still require hard work and dedication.

Before you spread yourself too thin, make sure you're getting involved with a side-hustle for the right reasons. Feel confident and prepared for the changes that are about to come in your life, and be ready for the feeling of empowerment that comes with thriving in a new business venture!

Chapter 2: What to Consider When Choosing a Hustle

Not every side-hustle is the perfect opportunity for everyone. Likewise, there are plenty of different types of gigs out there.

While side-hustles allow women to make more money on their own precious time, they don't differ too much from regular jobs. There is almost an infinite variety possible, and not every hustle will be a good fit for every woman. Just as not everyone has a desire to be a doctor or a lawyer, not everyone will be able to sell their own creative crafts or offer their in-home services... nor will they want to!

As you continue through this book, and even as you begin to peruse the internet to get a feel for some of the gigs that are available in your area, you'll want to be very conscientious about your wants and needs. It's important to remember that this is a form of a career, and you'll need to take it seriously. While you won't lose out on health insurance or a retirement plan if you quit, it's pretty disruptive to everyone involved if you suddenly have to back out due to this being an overall bad plan.

So, before you click on an advertisement, before you sign up for any net-working sites, before you even build a profile or start to consider creating a website, really think about the type of work you want to do.

Ask yourself the following questions:

1. Is this side-hustle interesting to me?

This is going to require true commitment. You will need to make sure you are going to be consistently capable of completing the tasks required in order to make a profit. Whether you have clients or customers, they will expect you to deliver what is requested within a specific time frame. If you choose something that you're only partially interested in, your motivation will wander off quickly. Instead, choose a side-hustle that keeps you inspired, and one that will hold your attention for hours at a time.

2. Is it lucrative?

Some side-hustles have a very low pay rate, but the more hours you work, the more money you make. When judging whether a gig is worthwhile, you want to measure the amount of time and energy you spend versus the amount of money you make. A simple job that makes $5 each time, yet only takes 15 minutes to complete will be more lucrative than a task that requires ten hours to complete, yet only pays $30 once you're done. The higher paycheck may sound tempting, but not when you realize that you could have completed the $5 job 40 times in the same ten hours, and made $200.

3. Will you be able to complete this gig regularly with your schedule or lifestyle?

Some side-hustles sound great on paper, but have a few more moving pieces than you expected. Because no two gigs are the same, you will need to do plenty of research, no matter which hustle you choose.

If you have a pretty predictable schedule, then this shouldn't be a problem. For many of us, life is unpredictable. There may be the odd day when you feel ill, or an unplanned emergency requires some fast thinking. Will your side-hustle allow you to drop everything and pick up a sick child from school? Can you put this gig on hold while you study for finals? If your day job has a busy season, will you want to follow up on deadlines and expectations after a super-long day?

Just because a gig sounds interesting and pays well, doesn't mean it's a great fit for where you are in life right now.

4. What is required from you?

Nearly every type of gig you can dream of will have a variety of demands. When investigating different options, you'll want to pay close attention to any requests that are specific to that option, in order to make sure that you're able to meet those expectations.

The most common requirements that you'll need to address are **time, travel, equipment, money,** and **space.**

When it comes to addressing **time requirements,** you'll need to know about deadlines. How many hours of work are required each week? What hours of the day should you be available? What time-sensitive tasks are involved, and are they on a regular schedule? Are there physical items which must be shipped or delivered? What type of turnaround time will you suggest for these items?

What about **travel requirements**? This is especially important to keep in mind if you're thinking of offering services like child care, house cleaning, pet sitting, and the like. How far are you willing to travel to provide these services? No matter how you choose to travel, commuting any distance will cost money. From bicycle tires to gasoline or a bus pass, your travel does involve some kind of investment. Will you roll that cost into your fees? What will you do if an ideal customer comes along, but they're just a smidge outside of the boundaries you set for yourself? Furthermore, will you be able to swing the commute with all of the other responsibilities you have, or will you be creating further mayhem in your schedule?

Then there are your **equipment requirements**. What will you need in order to successfully complete these gigs? You might regularly use a laptop, as well as certain programs, like Microsoft Office, or Adobe Photoshop. You might need to be part of a cloud network in order to share documents back and forth.

If you're taking on a creative endeavor, you'll need supplies in order to create. Every project comes with its own list of required tools and materials. Furthermore, if you're creating objects that will need to be shipped to customers, you'll have to investigate how to best package and ship them, which can be further materials you'll need to have on hand at all times.

You'll also need to think about how much **money** you have available to get things started. Equipment and travel considerations will all involve money at the outset, before you get paid for your side-hustle work. If you want to start a website to advertise your business, there will be domain and hosting fees, and you might need to hire a web developer to help you through unfamiliar territory. Does your side-hustle require you to take a few courses before you get started? What about insurance?

As the saying goes, you often need to spend money to make money. How much can you afford right now? How can you scale the process of establishing your side-hustle so that it makes sense within your budget requirements? While you may trick yourself into thinking "I can always make this money back!" That's not always true, especially if the side-hustle is a bust. Make sure you invest your money safely and wisely when starting a new gig, even if that means going a bit slower than you really wanted to go.

Lastly, what kind of **space** is needed in order to properly execute your side-hustle? This can include space in which to store all of your equipment. This could also consist of a private area where you can work on your laptop in peace. If you're creating something at home, what type of preparation space do you need? While a knitter might be able to complete a project in a comfy chair, a furniture repair side-hustle might require an entire workshop. Those with children or house pets will also want to be careful that the space in which they work on their side-hustle is safe from accidents, spills, or pet hair, too.

When you're considering a side-hustle, it's best to plan for the long-term. Though you may not be working on the gig you've chosen every day, you will be spending enough time on your efforts that you'll want to think all the way through the process. If you choose a task or project that leaves you feeling bored, rushed, underpaid, or underprepared, you might find yourself moving

131

onto another hustle quickly. This can lead to feelings of failure, disappointment, and depression.

Instead, walk through these questions for each gig you consider. This will give you a feel for how the day-to-day might work, but also the long-term investments of time, energy, and money. If, by the time you've gotten to the last question, you feel uncomfortable, overwhelmed, or disinterested, this is probably not the right side-hustle for you!

Chapter 3: The Early Stages of The Hustle

Before you jump in to claim your side-hustle, you must determine the rules for your particular hustle. You'll also need to begin marketing yourself, so that once you've got the wheels in motion, it will be much easier to work with potential clients. The process of marketing yourself has many steps, all of which we'll cover individually.

The goal in this stage is not to throw your hat into the ring, but to construct the perfect hat to throw into the ring once you've found gigs that meet all of your needs for the ideal side-hustle.

When it comes to full-time employment or a long-term career, we often have to settle for what's available. One beautiful thing about pursuing a side-hustle is that we call the shots. As women, we're frequently asked to do things above and beyond the scope of the job we were hired to do. When we conduct our own side-hustles, we have the ability to create all the boundaries, and now is the time to do so, before you contact your first potential lead.

Setting the Limits of Your Hustle

First, you'll want to examine your own personal boundaries. Now is the time to pull out your calendar, your class schedule, your children's activity schedules, and even your own sleep patterns, or things you like to do throughout the day.

Another piece of advice is to grab some paper and a pen so you can track your brainstorming process here. While you can start thinking about your limits anytime and all the time, such as when you're stuck in traffic, hitting a slow period in your day, the best way to commit them to reality is to write them down and plaster them somewhere prominent.

This is YOUR side-hustle. While your input into other jobs and tasks might be more passive, you are in control here. You establish the rules. You are creating your own business, where you're the boss. Now it's time to write your own employee handbook!

First, examine your schedule and create your availability. No matter what side-hustle you choose, in any industry, any skill set, or any product or service, people will demand more of your time than you can give. Before you get started, consider:

- When do you <u>want</u> to work?
- When <u>can</u> you work?
- What are you willing to sacrifice in the name of the hustle?

As you continue with this process, you may need to remind yourself of the following several times:

A side-hustle is not a full-time gig until I give it permission to be one.

Feel free to print this phrase out and post it somewhere very visible, such as on your refrigerator door!

What does this phrase mean? It means that you are in charge of your own destiny when it comes to your side-hustle. If your soap-making side-hustle takes off, for example, and you find it's very lucrative and brings you more joy than stress, then you might decide to give it your full-time attention. On the other hand, if you're finding your tutoring clients are texting you questions at all hours of the night, you might need to re-establish your limits. You are, after all, only one woman. The entire point of a side-hustle is to avoid spending all of your spare time working!

The process of setting limits continues. Next, you'll need to decide what you are and are not willing to do. True, you have not chosen your niche or your specific side-hustle yet, but there are things you need to define for yourself in terms of what you are and are not willing to sacrifice. For example, if a side-hustle requires you to work during a specific family event, are you willing to skip that event for the sake of income, or will you be willing to drop the side-hustle to be with your family?

Additionally, if you select a side-hustle that provides services, such as babysitting, tutoring, or house cleaning, what are some things you will not offer as part of your services? You should decide upon tasks that are within your skillset and comfort range. No matter what services you provide, you will always attract customers, but by limiting your services to what you can and will do, you will find yourself saying "no" more frequently. We'll explore that topic more shortly, but for now, make a list of things you can and cannot do, so that when future clients ask, you are prepared to draw that line in the sand.

The last part of the process when setting your limits regards pay. You will need to set your income requirements, as well as the minimum you can make in order to feel accomplished.

This number is subjective, so it is important to be realistic, especially at first. While we would all like to come out of the gate making five digits, it's not exactly practical. Instead, consider what a good starting hourly wage is for the talent and services you provide. Additional services may require extra payment. Quicker tasks might result in a lower per-task paycheck, but being able to do more quick tasks might result in a higher overall paycheck, as mentioned earlier.

If you're investing in materials for your side-hustle, such as in crafting or refurbishing items, you'll also want to pay attention to what you spend to create the end product. While you may purchase your objects, ingredients, and supplies in bulk for a lower cost, you are still spending money. Make sure you reimburse yourself not just for the effort and time that go into your side-hustle, but for actual monetary expenses, as well.

It can take over two years to prove yourself as an authority in your niche, so don't be surprised if the early months are very slow, and involve a lot of applications, conversations, and dead ends. The more experience you have, the stronger your reputation will become. In turn, the better your reputation, and the more referrals you receive, the higher the likelihood that you'll gain better-paying gigs through your side-hustle. Patience is a virtue, especially while establishing yourself in your new side-hustle.

Marketing Yourself and Creating Your Brand

When it comes to finding your groove in your side-hustle niche, you'll need to present yourself as a trusted authority. To do so, arm yourself with a variety of resources to share with potential clients, customers, or representatives.

Start this process by creating a profile for yourself and your business. You may not know where to upload this yet, but now is a great time to gather all of your thoughts about your experience, your talents, and the tasks you're willing to do, as defined in the last step.

One valuable resource to help you create your profile is LinkedIn. The goal of your profile is to share your credentials and build your online persona. You want to make sure you are relatable to others who view your profile, yet still show that you possess the experience necessary to serve as an expert in your field.

Step 1: Who Are You?

To get started, jot down some thoughts about yourself. Have others commented on your extreme attention to detail? Do you find yourself at ease when gathering and organizing information? Is time management definitely "your thing?" These are the type of details that will enhance your profile and lead to more possible side-hustle gigs.

Once you've honed in on the skill set you wish to use most in your side-hustle, think about some things you've done in your life related to that skill set. Remember- you're not applying for that huge corporate big-wig job. You're looking for a comfortable side-hustle that meets your needs, and that you can work on your own time.

Continue your brainstorming with some of these skills. They can include volunteer positions, one-day events, planning committees, and more. And **of course** you can use any relevant job skills! If, for example, you're a stay-at-home-mom who has experience in the job or field you're pursuing, absolutely include this information.

A profile is a little more intimate than the traditional resume, and more informal than the typical cover letter. Your goal is to present yourself as human, yet exceptionally talented and trustworthy. Rather than coming up with corporate-sounding terminology for your skills and abilities, you can be a bit more personal. This may sound a bit counter-intuitive to all of us women who have had to look "big and bold" on our professional resumes, but this actually will go a long way towards establishing your "boss lady" persona.

For example:

Instead of saying: *Starting in 2009, coordinated a team of 14 resources to research and develop a systematic process improvement for the company's implementation of a new time off policy, affecting a total of over 40,000 accounts.*

Try this: *I'm no stranger to having tough conversations. In 2009, my company implemented a new time off policy. My team of 14 skilled individuals and I put in many hours researching the best approach to share this new information with all of the company's 40,000 employees. We devised a strategy that allowed for personal discussions, with plenty of backup assistance from members of that team.*

The first example shows what you did, while the second shows how you did it. When you're making a profile for a side-hustle, keep in mind that the client or customer may not meet you in person for an interview. What they know about you comes strictly from your profile, followed by the conversations you have over email, Skype, or phone. Therefore, you want them to find you approachable and friendly right out of the gate.

How does this help with the "boss lady" persona? First, you'll establish trust. People who read an authentic, assertive profile will feel that you know what you're talking about, and that they can trust your assessment of a situation. Later down the road, when you need to discuss a difficult assignment or impossible deadline with them, they'll recognize that you're not just trying to weasel out of something- you have always been open and honest, and there's no reason to doubt you.

Additionally, they'll understand that you are a valuable resource. You're frank, and you don't need to hide behind self-important corporate lingo. You know what you did, and you're pretty darned proud of how it turned out. If they don't want your services, no problem- you'll find someone who meets *your* qualifications, not the other way around.

Regardless of whether you use LinkedIn or another service, you will want to create a profile that identifies your skills, your experience, your goals, and shows who you are as a person. Creating this document will be very helpful regardless of what side-hustle you choose. If you're starting your own business, you can post it on various employment sites, as well as your own website. If you're looking for freelance or contract work, you'll be able to load this profile to any job pool site, or send it to a prospective lead.

Step 2: Demonstrating Your Skills from Afar

If you are choosing a side-hustle that depends upon your skills, you might wish to create a portfolio. Here, you can display your previous work with samples or excerpts of relevant work.

The intention is not to present everything you've ever done, but some high-lights. If you're about to start a side-hustle doing commissioned artwork, for example, you won't need to show off photos of every single picture you've made. Though you are surely proud of all of your efforts, narrow down your collection to one or two examples of each type of media you will be selling.

This holds true for any type of creative work, including writing, photoshopping, voice work, and more. If your goal is to sell the work you create, show off the best of the best, rather than making prospective parties sit through a slideshow (or recording) of the evolution of your style. If you do several unique types of things, select the best of each. You can always offer to provide further examples upon request.

There are many types of side gigs where you may not be able to demonstrate your skills through virtual means. For example, it's hard to show people you're great at walking dogs through a website. In these cases, you'll want multiple references. You can display names, contact information, and professional reviews from those for whom you have worked in the past (with their permission, of course). In this case, you will want to have a handful of reviews available, so clients can learn more about the service you provide, and what to expect.

Building Your Boss Lady Brand

If you've ever worked in a corporate setting, or spent time in a business class-room, you've probably heard the phrase "You've got to build your personal brand!"

This phrase is especially true for women who are developing a side-hustle from the ground up. But what does it mean?

Take a look at all the companies out there advertising. Each has a very specific brand. From the logo, the slogan, the catch phrases, and the jingles, the goal of each company is to build a reputation through branding. The goal of the brand is to give customers a way to instantly recognize what the company is, what they're selling, and to establish them as the best possible option in their field. If you've ever gotten a jingle stuck in your head for a few hours, then you understand how companies use branding to stick with you!

As a woman looking to set up her side-hustle, you absolutely should do the same! Most of your personal branding is created through your profile, port-folio, and referrals, but you can also establish your brand virtually. This will ensure that everyone who views your information is aware of who you are, what you do, and gives them the feeling that you are confident and capable in your niche.

Consider using "I will" statements in a profile. "I will deliver (skill) to you in (timeframe)." Or "I will provide the desired results for (price)." You can also use these statements in your communications with customers.

Your brand is also reflected in how quickly you respond to messages, how well you communicate with the people who contact you about your side-hustle, your turnaround time for deliveries or shipments, and how you address and deal with any issues that might come up during your interactions. You may seem very capable, but no one will know this if they don't get the chance to connect with you.

This is why you spent so much time in the previous step, exploring your limitations. You will be able to communicate these to anyone with whom you work in your side-hustle to set the expectations for your brand.

If you identify as a top student who just needs a little extra lunch money during those final semesters, make this your brand. Make sure you're very clear in communicating that your education is most important to you, and that you will work around your important deadlines. You can do this in a friendly manner, with lines like *"As I work towards acing my final law exams, I'm also willing to take on a few tasks, such as (x,y,z). Please note that my classwork is my priority, so I will only be able to respond to inquiries after 6pm EST."*

How about busy mothers? The same advice applies. *"While I value our professional relationship, please note that my schedule can be hectic due to my children's needs. I will meet all pre-determined deadlines, but I may not respond to your messages right away."*

Establishing your brand means setting an understanding of what you can do, will do, and how you will do it. Your preferred contact methods, your schedule, and your abilities are all part of your brand.

Another thing to consider when marketing yourself for a side-hustle is your social media. Social media marketing is a huge part of any successful business in this day and age, and having a Facebook, Instagram, or Twitter page that reflects your ambitions in your side-hustle can be very important for communicating with and gathering an audience.

Bear in mind that your business profile is going to differ from anything you might currently have on social media. Your current social media pages might be a little more personal than what you wish to share with potential side-hustle contacts. The best idea is to make a business page for your more professional endeavors, strictly for side-hustle use. You can still keep your personal, fun social media outlets, but you should make a business-worthy page that strictly focuses on your side-hustle.

If you do make a social media page (or pages!) for your side-hustle, remember to keep them **strictly** professional. You may still wish to post jokes or memes, but make sure they apply to your business, and are in good taste. The general rule for "good taste" is posting only things you'd be willing to read in front of your entire family, your church, or in a court of law.

Marketing yourself, as mentioned before, is about establishing yourself as a trusted authority. Therefore, it's much wiser to post content on your social media pages that shares information about what you do, and industry related to your side-hustle, and details about your overall experience level.

If you're going to keep your own personal page to reflect your personal views and content, make sure you do not link it to your professional page. It is important to keep your personal life and professional life separate, especially when it comes to social media!

A Note: Being a Woman in Business-Driven World

The goal with this book is to avoid any cultural, social, or political drama. Around the world, there are many experiences between sexes and genders, so it would be very short-sighted to make generalizations about women and gender roles. That being said, it would be equally harmful to ignore the fact that two main stereotypes of women as business leaders exist.

First, there's the hard-as-nails, never-sleep, aggressive female who always gets what she wants. Recently, the term "Boss Lady" has been reclaimed from the allegedly negative stereotype. Society stereotypes women who focus on business as "cold," suggesting it is a bad decision for a woman, who is supposed to be warm and nurturing. As women, we are more than aware that we can think rationally and independently without sacrificing any compassion for others.

The second negative stereotype is the exact opposite- the pushover woman who runs a business seemingly for the sheer purpose of letting others take advantage of her. She always says yes and throws in extras. This stereotype is based largely on the notion that a kind, loving woman can't have significant business sense, because she relies on feelings, rather than intellect.

These are outdated and overplayed notions. Throughout the rest of this book, we will explore a variety of methods to keep you focused on running a successful side-hustle. The focus will be on logic, rational decisions, and open, honest communication.

It is equally important to acknowledge that emotions are part of the human experience. It's not just a "female thing"- everyone feels anxious, sad, frustrated, and elated at times. Through each step towards finding your new niche, we will highlight areas in which you might feel overwhelmed and emotional, and offer tips to help you confront that emotion and take it out of the equation.

Starting a side-hustle may take trial and error. You may need to stop what you're doing and regroup several times before you find your correct stride. You <u>will</u> become frustrated at some point in the process. You <u>will</u> make mistakes and forget deadlines. All of these actions and feelings you'll experience boil down to one main reality: **You are human.** Allow yourself to be human, and to express who you are in this world, but don't let these emotions overcome your sensibility in the business practice.

The early stages of the hustle can be the most promising, and the most frightening. You may feel very confident with the decisions you've made so far, but also somewhat terrified that things won't continue to go your way.

The truth is, both feelings are correct. The next steps of the process will be filled with uncertainty. You will need to work very hard and diligently to launch your side-hustle. By setting boundaries and creating your own personal brand, you are remaining true to yourself, your commitments, and your priorities. ·

You may feel some doubt as to how your side-hustle will happen, and how you will scare up business, but you are also very much on the way of living your best Boss Lady lifestyle!

SECTION 2:
GETTING YOUR HUSTLE ON

At this point, you are well-organized and prepared to jump into the process of getting your new side-hustle going. You may feel excited, apprehensive, or a little bit of both. But wait! We're not quite ready to open for business just yet!

Each step in the process of finding your ultimate side-hustle involves a lot of homework. In fact, as you'll learn later, the learning process never truly ends... unless you permanently shut down your business. Even then, you might find that the business mind never truly turns off.

Earlier, you brainstormed the skills that you bring to the table, as well as how much time, energy, and money you can devote to your new hustle. You should feel confident in everything that you've discovered about yourself. You should also have a new appreciation for all of your abilities and limitations. Take the time to look over the lists and ideas you've jotted down. Pay attention to the things that capture your attention repeatedly. These might be some key areas to focus on as you prepare your hustle.

While you do this, look for things that stand out to you as potential red flags. For example, let's say you wrote out "I'm great with customers," but the more you think of it, the more you realize you really, really don't like face-to-face interaction with others. Take it off your list! Change it! During this time, you need to be honest with yourself. That deep level of honesty is going to be reflected in the communications you'll have within your new role.

This is the stage where you hunt for a gig that reflects everything you can do, and works well within your requirements and limitations. You might be looking at your brainstorming notes, worried that there cannot possibly be a gig that meets your criteria. Rest assured, the opportunities are out there. In fact, you probably haven't even considered all of the options that exist!

The time has come to start looking around, so grab your notes, keep a copy of your profile, portfolio, and references nearby, and get ready to explore!

A Note: There Are So Many Side-Hustles- Explore Your Options

In this section, we'll look at many of the side-hustle options available to women today. This list is not meant to be all-inclusive. There might be a particular niche that's specific to your area. You might possess a creative talent that very few others share! This list should direct that Boss Lady energy into the right elements to help your side-hustle take off.

Reviewing this list should help you further organize your thoughts. Getting your ideas aligned will help you focus your energy towards opportunities, rather than plugging away at a situation that is just not working for you right now.

The hope is that, by reviewing these options, you start thinking of possibilities. In the "Resources" section at the end of this book, you'll find a variety of links that can help you get started with the search process. Perhaps, as you examine these leads, you'll think of something entirely different. Truly, that is the beauty of a side-hustle! As your own boss, you can explore anything that feels comfortable and suits your needs. Later, we'll discuss how you can use your experiences to continue to shape and grow your business, as well.

Chapter 1: Side-Hustles By Type

Before you rush into a side-hustle, take some time to discover what is available to you. That means looking near and far and doing a lot of research on the territories in between. The internet has opened up possibilities around the world, and it may turn out that someone on the other side of the planet is looking for exactly your skill set. On the other hand, your skills might fit right in your own backyard!

As stressed in the previous section, finding a side-hustle is all about finding something that works for you, that you're comfortable doing, and that helps you make the money you need. The following options are intended to offer inspiration and guidance for a variety of side-hustles that modern women pursue. It is not meant to be all-encompassing, but rather a starting point for you to create your own ideal Boss Lady business.

The Creative Types

If you have a talent for making or creating things, you can channel that talent into a side-hustle. This can take many shapes and forms; in fact, the beauty of being the creative genius of your own business is that you have control over all the aspects!

First, you can create your items and sell them via an online shop, or at various public venues, such as Farmer's Markets, Flea Markets, Swap Meets, or other bazaar-type settings in which crafters and creators gather to display and peddle their wares.

Examples of this include home made art and crafts, such as knitting or needlework, woodworking, painting or drawing, ceramics, jewelry making, quilting, soap making or creating bath goods, or any variety of mixed-media arts and crafts that you might enjoy.

This could also include culinary skills, too. Smaller dry-good items like gourmet popcorn, chocolates, cookies, fruit breads, or soup and dip mixes can be fun things you can create at home in your own time. It's easiest to market food that travels well, so while you might be extremely talented at creating three-tier gelatin molds, it might be hard to box those for the ride home. Plus, you'll want to take into consideration storage, weather at outdoor venues, and expiration dates. You will also need to look into local laws or regulations on production and sale of food-based items, depending on your area. That being said, people love to eat, and will likely be very eager to sample your creations.

Perhaps you'd like to help others learn to express their creativity. Channel your creative energy into teaching classes so others can learn from you. You might wish to take on individual students, or teach small classes, depending on the type of creation you'll be teaching.

You might have the opportunity to teach a paint night at a local winery, church, or women's association. Perhaps you invite some local folks to join you during after school hours to learn more about common knitting or quilting techniques while all of your students' children play together under your careful supervision.

Whether you are the "do-er" or the "teacher," your creative talents might be exactly the right starting point for your side-hustle. As you get started think about what you'd like to do, and how you plan on distributing your products. "Sewing" is a great starting point, but what will you sew? Where are you going to sell it? How will you package it? What materials do you need? There are going to be many moving pieces that you'll want to take the time to put together.

If you choose to use your creative talents as your side-hustle, you must keep very organized in order to keep your customers happy. This includes keeping track of all of your supplies, and knowing that they're all in good, working order at all times. This also means you need to know every step between your first idea to the customers' hands.

Here are a few examples of steps you'll need to keep coordinated in order to sustain your creative side-hustle:

Task	Requirements
Creating Product	1. Supplies 2. Time to create and finish 3. Space for creating product and allowing it to dry/cool/set
Distributing Product	1. Wrapping/ containers for product 2. Labels 3. Location 4. Website
Customer Service	1. Communicating available options 2. Custom orders? 3. Turn around time 4. Shipping time 5. Shipping costs 6. What if something goes wrong?
Things to keep track of	1. Incoming orders 2. Pending orders 3. Complete orders 4. What's in stock/ not in stock 5. Supplies

Let's briefly look at each of these in more detail.

Creating the product is actually the most straightforward part of this particular gig. You buy the supplies, make the item, and once it's complete, it's ready to sell to the customer.

KRISTINE HUDSON

The next step, distribution, is where things can get tricky. How will you get your creation into the customer's hands? If you make zucchini bread, for example, how are you going to package it so it stays fresh until it's consumed? If you're going to ship candles, how will you package them so they won't melt during transit?

You also must decide the route or routes through which you'll distribute your product to your customers. If you wish to set up a stand at a local festival or market, you'll need to pay the booth fee, and bring along any supplies that are not provided for you, such as tables, chairs, or tents. You'll also want signage that indicates what your product is, as well as ingredients or materials. Price tags and a way to take payment will be necessary, unless otherwise provided by the facility.

Another option is to sell your products through a website. In this case, you'll need clear, bright photos of all of your items, as well as product descriptions. You should include measurements, or ingredients, and make sure that customers are very clear on what they're purchasing. You'll need to make sure your site can process payments as you make sales, too.

You might prefer to sell through an established website for crafters. If you choose this route, make sure you're aware of any fees and guidelines from the site. Take note of whether you are required to pay commissions or listing fees. Check out seller rules to learn about shipping requirements or selling arrangements.

There's also the customer service aspect of this type of side-hustle. You need to be abundantly clear as to what you can and cannot provide. Many creative Boss Ladies like to offer only a few products at once, to save on overhead and to streamline the overall process.

You may wish to offer customers the option to request a customized order, too. Bear in mind that this will require you to purchase specific supplies to accommodate this order; however, you can include that cost in the amount you charge the customer. You'll also need to make sure you have enough time to complete this type of order as well as any other orders you might have coming in, so communication with customers with customized orders will be key.

If you're shipping your products, you'll want to determine how to communicate shipping times and shipping costs. This will require a bit of research to choose an appropriate mail carrier for your product, as well as their overall costs and delivery timelines.

You'll also want to decide how you'll work with customers if something goes wrong. Even in the most air-tight business model, things will get lost in the mail, or broken, or grow mold, or be defective in some way that will upset customers! Before you even get started, make sure you have a plan for these incidents, and be upfront with your customers about your policies.

Lastly, you'll want to keep immaculate records of your sales, supplies, and shipping details. These details are especially important when you run a business like this as a side-hustle, because you have much higher priorities in your life. Inevitably, real-life priorities, like a sick child, a class project that isn't turning out right, or extra hours at your full-time job, will interrupt the hours you had set aside to work on your products. If you keep very clear records, you'll be able to find where you left off without missing a beat. We'll look at some organization skills later in this book to help you get started.

Do you have a knack for finding a bargain? Are you the type who makes people jealous by walking into a department store and buying bag upon bag of awesome finds for just pennies on the dollar? You might be the right type of mastermind to run her own resale business.

The premise is quite simple: you find interesting items through shopping and then resell them via the internet, or through in-person venues, like craft markets, antique shops, or other gatherings, similar (or sometimes identical!) to those mentioned in the "Creative" section. Some people add value to the items they buy through cleaning them up or restoring them. Some take creative license to turn battered old furniture into one-of-a-kind collector pieces. You can also find new uses for old objects, like turning a bunch of used t-shirts into a quilt. The sky's the limit, but the ultimate goal is to take something old and of limited use into a highly desirable, functional item.

If this sounds like it's right up your alley, there are a few things you'll need to consider:

1. **Where will you source your items?** You can always check garage sales, thrift shops, flea markets, auctions, and more. Some ladies even have the imagination to turn items left on the curb as trash into stunning treasures! Remember: the less you spend on your finds, the more potential profit you can make.

2. **What will you do with them once you purchase/obtain them?** You'll need room to store things, and if you're bringing in items from garage sales or garbage bins, you might want to "quarantine"

them from the rest of your house until you've had the chance to properly clean them. If you plan to do any restoration or crafting, you'll also need a well-lit, ventilated space for this, and if you have children, an area where you won't have to worry about small fingers, sharp objects, or spills!

3. **How will you price them?** You'll need to research the items you sell to make sure you're charging the right amount. They say that everything is only worth as much as someone will pay for it, so you'll want to make sure you put just the right price tag on your items so that people will buy them AND you can make a profit. If you're putting any work into the item, you'll want to make sure you're compensated for your time and any supplies, as well.

4. **How will you sell them?** Sites like eBay, Craigslist, and Etsy are typical go-tos for women in the resale business, but you might want to explore other options. Perhaps you have a local craft or flea market that would be perfect for the objects you resell. Maybe you find yourself with a surplus of items and wish to start your own website to sell what you've got. If you choose to sell online, you'll need pictures of your items to accompany your ads.

5. **How will you deliver them?** If you sell through a local shop, this part is taken care of for you. But if you're selling your products online, you need to make sure you have a way for customers to get their purchases. For example, if you restore an antique oak wardrobe, the shipping costs might be phenomenal, but local pickup would be fairly easy for a person with a truck. Keep this in mind when listing your objects!

Besides answering all of these questions, you'll still need to keep very detailed records of what you've purchased, when you purchased it, and when it was sold. Keep detailed inventory so you don't accidentally double-sell something, and to ensure you don't let the buying get out of control. Shopping for resale can be fun, especially if you enjoy shopping, but you want to make sure you're shopping sustainably. That is, don't buy more than you can sell, and if something isn't selling, you might need to readjust your methods and techniques!

It is wise to make sure there's a market for an item before you invest your money in buying all you can find. While you might find a certain aesthetic, type of clothing or jewelry, or household object fascinating, you aren't buying for you- you're SELLING for you! Do your homework before you buy so you know what you want to sell, and where you plan to sell it. Otherwise, you might have your own garage sale soon!

The Freelancer Life

You've probably heard the term "freelance" kicked around a time or two, but you might not have taken the time to explore what it means until now.

The terms and conditions of a freelance relationship vary between the parties involved, and the term "freelance" has become more of an umbrella term for a relationship in which one party completes a project for another in exchange for payment, but they are not officially an employee of the paying party.

The types of gigs available to freelancers vary, but typically involve a specific skill or talent. If you have experience with writing, photography, web design, online marketing, voice work, or digital art, you might want to explore the world of freelance in more detail.

Each niche has a plethora of possibilities:

- Writers of fiction, non-fiction, web content, press releases, research specialists, grant writers, scriptwriters and more can find options.

- Photographers and videographers of all styles and editing types can be engaged for special occasions, family portraits, band photos, corporate events... for every important event in life, someone needs to be there to capture every moment!

- Web designers and site builders can be utilized to build, edit, and re-design a variety of websites, from small, simple tasks, to complete overhauls.

- The marketing realm of freelancing can be expansive, from brand designers, to media updates, to social media experts and beyond.

- Those with golden voices can read audio books, provide translations, and offer voiceover work, just to name a few options.

- Digital artists can design logos, create media for websites, provide whiteboard video content, or extensive editing, among other options.

If you have any expertise in these areas, you might make freelance work your side-hustle. There are plenty of options beyond those listed, but all fall under the same umbrella. The basic premise of freelancing is that you are not an official employee, but you are getting paid for short-term, temporary work.

There can be a lot of grey areas in freelance work, so it's important to fully research every gig and make sure you're aware of your rights and requirements. Here are a few things to be aware of when investigating freelance opportunities:

- Some hiring parties do not require a contract to be signed by either party. On one hand, that can be helpful if you need to disengage from the person who hired you. You aren't required to give notice, and you aren't obligated to complete anything. Naturally, it's preferable to act professionally, but this scenario applies to more emergency-based situations. At the same time, the person who hired you isn't obligated to pay for any work they don't like. Without a contractually agreed upon assignment, they can ask you to do something over and over again... and you can't stop them from using anything you've sent them. So, always double check the terms of your agreements.

- Frequently, people who hire freelancers expect to get more than they pay for. As someone who takes pride in your talents and abilities, you might have a strong drive to impress the people who hire you. Make sure they pay you for all of your efforts (more on being an effective Boss Lady in a bit!).

- Generally speaking, you will never get credit for what you produce as a freelancer. This might be perfectly fine for you. After all, you know what you produced, and you were paid adequately for your efforts. All is right in the world! However, you may be very restricted on your ability to claim that work as your own. Naturally, you can never publish something that you've created for a client, but you might be able to use excerpts or samples of your work for a future portfolio. Always ask before you do so.

There are many freelance sites that work to specifically connect freelance workers with potential clients. These gigs can include long-term projects, in which you set up a working relationship for months or years with a client, and very quick assignments, such as sprucing up a quick landing page, or rewording a short "about" paragraph. In the resource section, you can find more detailed information about these types of sites, which include Upwork, Fiverr, Craigslist, Mechanical Turk, and more.

Online Options

The internet is a huge place, and there are tons of opportunities for people who are willing to put forth the time and effort.

Sometimes, you'll find there is a bit of overlap between online gigs and freelancing, as most freelancing opportunities have a large email/virtual component to them. There are quite a few options that require a unique skill set, however.

For example, online tutoring is quickly gaining popularity. From helping small children learn basic math, to assisting adults attempting to learn a new language, the skills and knowledge you have might be exactly what someone else needs to boost their understanding. There are a variety of tutoring sites available that can connect potential tutors with students. We have listed a few in the "Resources" section at the end of this book.

Typically, these services require tutors to demonstrate their knowledge of various subjects, so you may be asked to not only submit your profile and portfolio, but to take a few tests on the topic you intend to tutor. A client may ask you to conduct a few test sessions, or complete their structured training on the preferred style or software used for the tutoring sessions. Before you get started, make sure you're fully aware of all of the requirements, including the steps of the process, the equipment/software required, the expected results, and the pay scale. Otherwise, you could end up in an unexpected bind, scrambling for a webcam or trying to find a way to make the schedule work.

Resume writing is another online service that is gaining popularity. Some people have the special ability to create a resume that captures the attention of employers right away, communicating all the necessary skills without sounding too cold, too unprofessional, or too casual. If that sounds like you, there are plenty of people who could use your help!

In most cases, dusting up a resume or making recommendations for a cover letter is not time consuming. You can handle tasks like these after homework, after dinner, or before the kids get up for school. It can also be a significant way to exercise your language talents, Human Resources experience, or skills you learned in business classes.

If you're very good at keeping things organized, check out virtual assistant opportunities. This position is often crucial for new and small business owners, who need help with certain tasks, but can't afford to have someone on board full-time to handle these tasks. Often, a virtual assistant will help with remote tasks, such as managing social media accounts, keeping calendars updated, responding to general emails, and providing updates to clients, but these are just a few of the tasks that virtual assistants might do.

For example, a virtual assistant may be tasked with setting reminders to the business owner's calendar so they receive an alert for due dates and appointments. They may also do the legwork for researching local opportunities to expand the business. This can also include making basic inquiries, such as to a real estate company for a shopfront, followed by scheduling appointments for the owner to speak to the real estate agent. Your duties might include determining what the next steps are for various opportunities, based on research you conduct, and communicating them to the business owner. Sometimes this includes customer service functions, such as responding to emails or online requests.

Astoundingly, you may never meet your employer. They may not even live in the same country! In fact, there is a segment of the market interested in bi-lingual assistants, so if you are fluent in multiple languages, you might find a gig as a virtual assistant very quickly. Just make sure all parties involved are aware of time differences, especially when making appointments or sending urgent communications.

Another newer type of virtual side-hustle is email marketing and affiliate marketing. These are unique opportunities for those who have a lot of internet savvy. Many online companies do not have permanent marketing departments, so they contract a lot of the work out to others, especially those tasks which are fail-proof, but take up time and energy that the owners of these companies simply do not have.

Email marketing is a process in which you, as the marketer, contract with someone who is selling a specific product or service via a website, to write and distribute emails for them. Before you get too involved, you'll want to make sure that this company is legitimate, and learn the details of their marketing program. There are plenty of things that are not ok in the world of email marketing. For example, signing someone up for email newsletters without permission, or buying lists of emails online. You don't want to accidentally fall into a situation that is illegal!

In a legitimate campaign, the vendor gives you access to an email site, or simply asks you to write copy and submit it to your contact at the company directly. This can include writing emails for sales, newsletters, or regular updates. They may even give you the copy and ask you to format it, edit it, and distribute it. Payment typically comes in the form of a commission, when the email recipients perform the action desired, such as clicking a link, making a purchase, or using a coupon code.

Affiliate marketing is a recent phenomenon. Affiliates contract with companies who sell products or services, just as email marketers do. They are given their own link or code, and then receive specific instructions for marketing strategy, or they have the opportunity to place advertisements using their codes across the internet, at their own expense. When someone clicks on the ads the affiliate has placed, in order to sign up for a newsletter, get a quote, or make a purchase, this is tracked by the company selling the product or services. The company will then pay the affiliate in commissions for their role in energizing business through online marketing.

This may not seem lucrative, but consider that placing ads on Facebook, for example, can be very inexpensive. If you run a blog or YouTube channel of your own, mentioning the company for whom you are an affiliate is absolutely free. If you can convince your audience to click on your specific link, you'll make a commission off of the purchases they make.

For the most part, these marketing opportunities call for plenty of research when you get started, to better understand the niche in which you are working, and to learn the expectations of the company contracting you. Once you've got your ads in place, however, you only need to keep an eye on how well the ads are performing, and readjust your strategy as necessary to make sure your ads are visible, and that large numbers of people are clicking on them.

There are free classes available online for those who are interested in marketing from home. While the term was previously associated with more nefarious and less legitimate practices, bear in mind that many large companies, such as eBay, Amazon, and Target, offer affiliate marketing programs for individuals. With the advent of services like SendInBlue and MailChimp, for example, email marketing is now much more controlled, allowing recipients of emails to unsubscribe and remove themselves from lists at any time. As a result, these marketing techniques are less a nuisance, and more geared towards individuals who are truly interested in the goods and services provided by the companies who contract the marketers.

Another type of side-hustle that ties in with these is blogging. The main draw to blogging is that you can write about whatever you want, whenever you want. The money comes from allowing advertisements on your blog, or acting as a social media influencer for various brands.

The first step to becoming a blogger is determining what you want to write about. While you might have a few very keen passions, research a few different niches before you choose one, to determine what types of blogs are most current and frequently updated, and what you might do to make your blog special. After all, you'll get noticed by standing out from the crowd!

You may want to with some of your hobbies and brainstorm ways you can work in relevant advertising. In most cases, you'll need to reach out to various companies to find out if they're willing to coordinate with you as an affiliate or influencer through your blog. They will ask to read your blog and get a feel for your following, as well. Therefore, you'll want to make sure you hit the ground running with unique, authoritative content, interesting visuals, and a robust social media presence.

This might seem like a lot of effort but once you get all of these details aligned, your gig will require only maintenance, going forward. Plus, this is another type of task you can work on any time you have a spare fifteen minutes, jotting down notes and drafting ideas, and not submitting final versions until you've had a while to put everything together!

If you love cooking, for example, you can put together some recipes, especially those that you have come up with yourself, or learned from family members. You might include video of making the recipe, or photos of the process. Perhaps you can reach out to various name brands of ingredients or cookware companies for potential sponsorships or ad opportunities. Create a Facebook page for your blog, with links to other local food groups, national cooking stars, and product pages. This will help establish your credibility in your niche.

Earlier, we discussed transforming a hobby into a side-hustle, such as crafting, needlework, and more. A blog is a great way to take that creative side-hustle to the next level without sacrificing your spare time. While the paint dries, the cakes cool, or you wait for the next farmer's market to come around, you can take some time to discuss your projects or processes via a blog.

Consider writing out your options so you don't lose track of your plans. You might chart out your blog concepts, thoughts for future entries, as well as to whom you might contact for advertising opportunities.

See how many concepts and ideas you can come up with each time you visit this chart. For example, your chart might include a few wildly different topics:

Blog Concept	Entry Ideas	Sponsors?
Adventures in Parenting	Activity ideas, road trip ideas, snacks, back to school preparation	Local kids' spots, foods marketed to children, car seat companies, children's footwear, school supply sales ads
The Trials and Tribulations of Being a Working Student	How to find time to study, balancing work, class, and having a life, organizational tips	Laptops/tablets/devices, apps for motivation/activity tracking, organizational tools/apps, local coffee shops
At Home Wine Making	The process, where to find supplies, recipes, fun varietals	Equipment distributors, juice makers, other small/independent wineries, crafters who make wine-related accessories

These are just a few examples to demonstrate the process. Your mind may go in a completely different direction, and that's when you'll know your blog is unique!

Remember, the path to success with a blog is paved with viral content. Think of all the times you've shared or had a blog post shared with you. You want people to read your posts, but then you want them to keep reading, and keep sharing. The more readers, the higher the likelihood of clicks on the ads run on your page, which keeps your commission coming in!

Online options are unique, because there is a strange balance of "hands on" and "hands off." In tutoring, for example, you only have the time of your appointment to connect with your student and offer insight, but what they take away with the interaction can be the help they need to achieve great success. A virtual assistant may just set up appointments, but those meetings can lead to unimaginable business growth for the owner of the company. Marketers may create ads and emails, but when their laptop is closed, someone may click on their ad and discover a solution to a problem that has been bothering them for a long time. Through minimal contact, you are making a significant impact!

In-Person Services

Nearly all of us have said, "Oh, if only I had someone to help me with... ." As your side-hustle, you could be that someone!

There are many opportunities to provide direct services to others in your area. People who have homes or offices often need help with cleaning. Busy moms and dads might need help from someone who can watch and entertain their children from time to time, or help with tricky schoolwork. Those who have pets are frequently looking for someone to help keep their furry family members groomed, exercised, and safe and sound while they're out of town. Cars need washing and lawns demand constant attention.

Depending on the time and skills you have available, you might be able to make a nice side-hustle out of cleaning, babysitting or tutoring, pet sitting, car washing, or yard work. Like any side-hustle, there will be plenty of pros and cons:

Pros	Cons
You set your own schedule	There can be long "dry spells" where you won't have any customers
You get to choose where you work	You will have to commute to the job site
You can always decline a customer for any reason	Turning down a customer too many times may cause them to find someone else
You don't have to pay fees or commissions	You'll most likely have to purchase all of your own supplies and carry them to and from the job site
You set the terms for what you will or won't do	The customer may not like your efforts

Chances are good that you've helped people with this type of service before, in which case, you are aware of the potential perils and pratfalls. Once this becomes your actual side-hustle, though, you might feel additional pressure to perform well, since you're depending on this income to help you out.

You might also need a special license, permit, or certification for these types of gigs, depending on where you live. Make sure you check out the regulations for independent services in your area before you advertise or take on clients. You don't want to find yourself in legal trouble due to an accidental oversight!

It is also a good idea to ask your insurance agent what the local guidelines are for those who provide in-home services to others. The term "liability" means something different around the world, but no one wants to engage in a legal battle with a client about who is at fault for an accident or mishap. Take the time to sit down with your agent or a legal advisor to make sure you are fully informed of your responsibilities and those of your clients. They may not be aware of the local laws, either!

There are also several types of in-person jobs that are directly regulated by a specific company or contractor. For example, you might drive for a rideshare company like Uber or Lyft, or a food delivery service in your spare time. These types of jobs require a reliable vehicle, however, so make sure you've got a clean car in working order before you apply.

Another option of an in-person service is Mystery Shopping. These types of jobs are usually interactive, but you can do them at your own pace, usually within a certain amount of time. The company requesting the mystery shop asks you to go to a restaurant or store during specific hours. You may have a particular task to perform, or the requesting company may ask you to do what you would normally do in that location. You'll then complete a report and send it back to the company that requested the review.

A Word About Keeping your In-Person Side-Hustle Safe and Healthy

When you engage in an in-person side-hustle like these, make safety your number one priority. Women are often considered "easy targets" for criminals. Make sure someone always knows where you are, and that you have emergency contacts lined up at all times. You need to be aware of your own location, especially if you are driving to an unfamiliar area. There's no reason to live in fear, but practicing general awareness when meeting new clients is always a good idea.

Taking self-defense classes is an excellent idea for all women, regardless of age, background, or type of side-hustle. It's also wise to practice basic safety habits at all times, including using the buddy system after dark, making sure you're aware of all points of entry or exits, and being fully aware of your surroundings. These common sense techniques can keep you alive in worst case scenarios.

Your physical and mental health are also extremely important. You might have to remind yourself to not overextend yourself with these side-hustles. Cleaning houses, for example, is a very physical activity. Make sure you allow your body enough time to recover after washing dozens of high windows or walking a large, rambunctious dog. The goal of a side-hustle is that it doesn't interfere with your daily life, and while it's inevitable that some conflict will come along, you want to remain as physically and mentally ready for the challenges of your routine as ever. If you notice you're going to the massage therapist or chiropractor more often as a result of your in-person gig, or if you are stressing about when you'll finish your homework (or help your kids with their homework!) you're likely over-extending yourself.

You can mitigate some undue stress on your body and mind by making sure you take on clients slowly. Whether you're pet sitting, babysitting, cleaning houses, driving a rideshare, or doing Mystery Shops across town, don't jump in headfirst. Unlike the gigs that you can do from your own home, most of these in-person side-hustles will take place during daytime hours, and can't be postponed until the kids are in bed, for example. Give yourself plenty of breathing room as you get started, and if you find yourself outside of your comfort zone, remember that you, as the Boss, have the right to reschedule and dial back on customers' expectations. It may take a few months to find your stride, but eventually, you'll discover a balance that makes everyone happy.

Some women swear by the success they have found with Multi-Level Marketing companies, or MLMs. These are companies that encourage women to come aboard as consultants, selling a variety of products. Mary Kay, Avon, Beachbody, and Scentsy are some of the most popular MLMs on the market today, but there are many more opportunities available.

In order to make a profit, those who work as consultants for MLMs are encouraged to market their products to their own contacts, either through their own social media, hosting gatherings, or creating personal websites. They are also encouraged to recruit other individuals to branch off and start their own business as a consultant. Consultants make money off of commissions from sales, as well as for bringing on additional downstream team members.

If there is a product you enjoy, and have friends that will buy large quantities of this product on a regular basis, joining an MLM might not be a bad idea. However, many companies require newcomers to invest in a significant amount of their products to sell in person. They may stipulate that you meet specific sales quotas before you see any profit. Your friends may not use the product in big enough quantities, or need these items as quickly as you must meet these sales quotas, either, leaving you with a ton of surplus items and little profit.

In order to succeed with an MLM, you will need to constantly market to a larger and larger group of people. It can be done, of course, as evidenced by the over 24,000 people who are driving Mary Kay's coveted Pink Cadillac. Still, this is not a hands-off commitment. You will need to make the sales figures, you will need to market your product endlessly, and you will need to continuously build your sales team.

As with any side-hustle, it's important to read all the rules and regulations of a Multi-Level Marketing company before you sign up. As marketing specialists themselves, the top tier individuals in the company will do an impressive job of making the opportunity sound as enticing as possible. If everything aligns with your goals, make sure you have the startup capital, as well as the time, energy, and resources to market your product.

And That's Not All!

These are, as mentioned previously, just a few of the examples of side-hustles available for women today. This list, along with the links in the "Resources" section, should get your creative juices flowing, allowing you to brainstorm and consider what types of tasks may fit your lifestyle perfectly.

Chapter 2: Do the Research

At this stage, you've got a few potential options in mind for your side-hustle. Now, how do you get started from here?

Starting a side-hustle is, in all intents and purposes, starting your own small business, no matter which gig you pursue. You'll have to market yourself, including getting the word out about what you do, who you are, what you charge, and why people want to choose you over anyone else. Then, make sure you've checked out the legal and financial requirements of the gig, as well as any licensing or insurance requirements. You need to analyze what you can offer, how you offer it, and your overall goals and boundaries.

Getting the word out about your side-hustle will be a constant need in order for your business to thrive and survive. This is why you spent time on creating your profile and portfolio earlier. In some cases, this may be as simple as posting your profile and portfolio on a contracting or connection site, as with freelancing and tutoring sites, for example. The people who use those sites will already be on constant lookout for people who provide the skills and talents you bring to the table, so they'll come across your information organically.

For other types of gigs, however, you may need to start your own website and start tooting your own horn, so to speak. Now is the time to place those ads on Craigslist and local Facebook sites. Load your profile and portfolio to professional sites such as LinkedIn. Create your own professional social media profiles and websites.

Before you launch your very own side-hustle business, you need to define a few parameters, so make sure you've done some essential Boss Lady research.

What's The Catch?

If you're going to create an account with a third party site, such as Craigslist, Etsy, eBay, Fiverr, or Upwork, make sure you read all the fine print first. Before you start excitedly loading ads and pictures, make sure you've captured all the details.

For example, are there any fees associated with posting on the site. Some of these sites allow users to post a profile free of charge, but they may charge a commission, or require a bidding process to gain a client. On others, you might be required to pay a monthly subscriber fee or "exhibition fee" for posting your wares or services on the site. Make sure you're aware of your financial obligations before you get started. It's also imperative to do the math- if a site costs $30 a month to host your shop, and you only plan on doing a little bit of work here and there as your schedule permits, does your income balance this fee? While it's true that you might have to spend a little to earn a lot, you shouldn't be spending more than you make!

What's Your Part In It?

Aside from your financial responsibilities, what other guidelines must you follow? For those working directly with clients, this is a conversation that you will have with each customer directly. For those working through a third party, either by selling goods and services, or contracting various jobs, there might be requirements from that site.

As an example, some sites might want workers to obtain certain quotas in sales per month. Some may request a specific level of job approval, typically through positive ratings from previous gigs. Make sure you plan strategically to meet those requirements. Generally speaking, those goals are intended for people doing full-time work, and as a side-hustle, your hours will be far less. Make sure the goals are attainable before you fail to meet them out of sheer lack of time.

What's the Market Like?

Another important area of research is getting a sense of how your niche operates. This means exploring not only your tasks and skills, but the area of the world in which you aim to do it.

KRISTINE HUDSON

You will need to understand who the competition is, regardless of the side-hustle you choose. If there are 400 babysitters available in your town of 10,000 people, the competition will be fierce. You'll need to draft a business plan that is competitive and adds value that the other babysitters in your town don't provide. On the other hand, perhaps there are only a few people who do what you do. Find a way to reach out and network with these individuals before you dive in. If they're so swamped, they can't keep up with demand, be wary- this is the sort of situation in which a side-hustle can become overwhelming very quickly. The flip side is that these few people might be completely bored and running out of ways to drum up business, in which case you might want to re-examine your side-hustle plans.

What you're looking for is a nice balance- a sweet spot in which there is definitely demand for your intended side-hustle, but not so much that you're figuratively jumping into a pool full of piranha... or a completely empty pit! You want to make sure that you have a market and get to know that market. This may involve looking for some local Facebook groups, networking with others in your field, and checking out some online shops or groups in your niche. The goal is to be fully prepared the minute you open your virtual doors.

As you look around for others who provide a similar service, get a feel for what they provide, as well. Check out their profiles and portfolios, and start brainstorming not how you can be like them, but how you can differentiate yourself from them. Everyone has their own preferences and specialities. What will make your side-hustle more successful for you is that it is individual to you. The more your efforts honestly reflect your skills and talents and preferences, the more customers will appreciate your dedication and integrity.

Take the time to review your profile and your portfolio. What are some things you do that set you apart? It can be the handwritten note you leave thanking your clients for their business, or your knowledge of a particular style or technique. What additional skills do you have that enhance your abilities and really draw you to this particular side-hustle?

These are the added touches that will bring attention to your business, and will undoubtedly boost your side-hustle's growth. We'll talk more about how to build a customer base in the next chapter, but before you get to that step, you must have your identity and skills established within your side-hustle. If that means taking a few quick online courses to brush up your knowledge, or devoting serious time to considering fun things you can do to put your own trademark on your work, now is the chance to explore and nail down these options.

What Should You Charge?

Another factor you need to consider before you at last commit to your chosen side-hustle is what your rates will be. Ideally, you'll want to receive enough payment to cover your materials/supplies and travel (if any), as well as your time and effort, and make a little profit. Your goal is to make a return on investments, and a bit extra.

The first step to knowing what to charge is to understand your financial goals. How much do you need to make each week? How many gigs can you take on, or how regularly do you expect to receive compensation? What are your overall objectives, and the timeline in which you need to reach your goals?

This looks very different for every woman. You may feel pretty satisfied at the prospect of breaking even, but for many women, a side-hustle is a way to earn extra money in her spare time, which means structuring rates in order to create a profit. That profit might set aside for one particular thing, such as paying college tuition for yourself or your children. You might wish to apply it to a future down payment on something huge, like a car or a house. Alternately, you might just like having a few extra bucks each week to satisfy a particular splurge. These are all perfectly fine reasons to engage in a side-hustle, and they help you calculate both the volume of income you need, and how quickly you intend to reach that total.

Once you've figured out your personal needs, it's time to look back into the community to see what the typical rates and charges look like for your side-hustle.

This is another area where it literally pays to do your research. By now, you've reviewed other profiles and products of those in your niche, so you have a good idea of what they do, how they do it, and what they charge.

You may wish to keep your rates in the same ballpark, at least at first. Though you are confident that your specialized way of performing the required tasks sets you apart from the competition, you may not want to start out with prices that those who have not experienced your service might find ludicrous. The potential issue with this pricing model is that you may not be able to increase prices on existing clients, once word starts to circulate and you build your stellar reputation.

Another option is to offer different packages. Contracting sites such Fiverr use this model, along with many in-person services. It is a great way to interactively set rates. For a certain price, you'll be able to complete a certain number of tasks. For a higher rate, you'll add specific elements, or elevate the experience.

Here are a few examples of how that can work for various side-hustle opportunities:

Type of Job	Package A	Package B	Package C
Pet Sitting	3 check-ins, including meals, water, and one walk.	Full-time overnight care, including all meals, water, walks, and medication. Complete report of food/water intake, bathroom activities, and behavior notes.	Full-time overnight care with meals, water, walks, medication, nail trimming, and basic grooming (brush or bath). Complete report of food/water intake, bathroom activities, and behavior notes.
Resume Writing	Review existing resume, report recommendations within 24 hours.	Review existing resume, including all recommendations via word doc editing tool, within 48 hours.	Create new resume based on client's reported skills and experiences, tailored for a specific job application. Basic cover letter included. Turn around time of 48-72 hours.
Quilt Making	Pre-made quilts available for sale in a variety of colors, sizes, and patterns. Available to ship immediately.	Custom quilts made based on color and size preferences. Turn around time based on size and shipping requirements.	Custom quilts based on fabric requests. Size, thickness, pattern, all to customer's request. Turn around time discussed in full based on scope of project.

Naturally, the options you provide will depend upon your skills, and will be tailored to your particular side-hustle. These are just a few examples to get your thought process started on how to make your business unique, valuable, and profitable.

One very important thing to note at this stage of planning is that even the best-laid plans change. As you gain experience with your side-hustle, you might start branching out, adding services, or not offering certain options any more. This is not only acceptable- it's encouraged! Always take the time to remind yourself that this is a side-hustle. If you find it taking more time than you have to offer, re-strategize. Should you find the amount of work you provide doesn't align with the pay you receive, review your plan. In case you find that people want one package more than the others, make that your standard offering, and offer other options only upon request.

Being a Boss Lady, you are entitled to update your business plan whenever the need arises. This ensures you're staying on top of your primary priorities. After all, your kids will only be little for so long. Your professors aren't going to be impressed if you fail the big midterm paper because you were writing articles for a client. And your spouse probably won't be thrilled if you're out tending to everybody else's lawn while your home is slowly engulfed in a jungle.

As you're designing your packages and coming up with your rates, make sure you're really paying attention to what you can reasonably do in each scenario. If an option or add-on will cost you more money or time you don't have- don't offer it. You want your rates to be competitive, and you want to cover expenses with a little left over, and you don't need to go too far out of your way to justify your rates.

A Note: Is All This Research Necessary?

You may have friends or family members who just decided one day to have a side-hustle. They sat down at their laptop or creative station, and ta-da! They've made a tidy little income for themselves, and they didn't have to do all this research and back work. So why do we keep recommending you look into things and do research?

The truth is that side-hustles are more popular than ever. Many people have discovered ways to work for themselves, which means any niche you can dream of is more competitive than ever. Doing the leg work before you get started is intended to save you a lot of heartache, a lot of stress, and unnecessary time spent trying to make something work. You will discover whether a side-hustle is a good fit or not during this preliminary work, before you've become emotionally or monetarily connected to it.

As women, we often feel the pressure to be superhuman. We're used to doing whatever it takes to make things work. We're often challenged with fixing things, saying "yes" to everything, and over-extending ourselves to avoid disruption of the status quo. Do not let your side-hustle be the straw that breaks the camel's back. A side-hustle should always be fun and low-stress.

Being successful at your side-hustle shouldn't take away from your ability to be a parent, a student, a partner, or a professional in another career. This is why we keep emphasizing that a side-hustle should only be a full-time gig if you want it to be. With so much competition these days, you may feel pressured to extend yourself, which we'll deal with in the next section. Many women can share stories of side-hustles gone sour due to thousands of bad situations. The goal of encouraging this research is to make sure you're standing firmly on your feet as you wade into unfamiliar territory.

Chapter 3: Landing the Gig

Alright. So you've at long last chosen your side-hustle. You've figured out what different options you offer and how you will do what you do best. You know when you can work, and what you will charge for each task. Now the time has come to put yourself out there and get that hustle!

When people are starting a new gig, they might be tempted to use the phrase "I'll just dip my toes in and see what it's like." There's a lot of truth to that phrase- it can take significant time to build up a customer base, which we'll discuss shortly. At the same time, you may have chosen a very in-demand niche. When you start dabbling in your side-hustle, you should be ready to go immediately.

That means that if you're a creative type, you've already got your supplies and shipping materials. Resalers have some items that can be shipped or picked up tomorrow. Freelancers and virtual ladies have their laptops fired up, software loaded and at the ready. In-person services have all of their supplies waiting at the door. MLM gals have their catalogues, order forms, and samples present and ready to share. Every last one of us needs to know their rates, their restrictions, and their requirements before hitting the "Send" button.

Why do you want to be at the ready? Because while rare, we all know that one woman who put out an ad and got a response in minutes, as mentioned in the last "A Note" section. While it's unlikely, it does happen. There's nothing wrong with turning down a gig because it's not a suitable fit, but it's hard to recover when you have to turn down a gig because you aren't ready! If you say you've got an antique spinning wheel for sale, resale Boss ladies, then don't respond to inquiries with "Well, I still have to paint it, and it's been in my garage for a few months, so I might need to do some repairs... ." Getting prepared and doing the research mentioned in the previous chapters takes time, but don't jump the gun by potentially attracting customers before you're prepared.

This goes for upcoming vacations or busy days, as well. If you know you have a packed schedule on the horizon, or for an extended period of time, wait until that's passed before you work on preparations for your side-hustle. Yes, it is very exciting, and it's understandable to want to get everything posted and ready right away, but don't press yourself into a corner before you even get started!

Once you're ready, take several deep breaths and get ready to land your first gig in your new side-hustle!

Step 1: Market Yourself

In order to gain customers, clients, and gigs, you're going to have to put yourself out there. Earlier, you wrote a profile and portfolio. That helped you understand where you wanted to apply your skills, talent, and knowledge. Organizing your details beforehand also helped you fine-tune what you plan to offer within the realm of your side-hustle and has set you on a path to complete your research before you hopped onto the market.

Before you move forward, take one last look at your profile and portfolio to tweak any details that might have come to mind while you were doing your research. Once you feel satisfied that you have given your best effort, and that your business is accurately reflected, the time has come to send it out into the world!

Depending on the type of side-hustle you choose, joining online groups related to your hustle is a quick and easy first step. This can include any Facebook groups, LinkedIn communities, local selling/buying walls, or online forums that feature your niche. Not only will this help you get a better understanding of the current vibe and events related to your side-hustle, but many people are eager to network with and provide mentorship for others who are just getting started.

Next, start looking at ads and postings, on local sites, or Craigslist, or on networking/contracting sites within your type of gig. Be certain you have read each posting carefully, and don't try to make a round peg fit in a square hole, so to speak. You are likely very keen to get started, with a certain adrenaline rush every time you get a new email, but make sure you're able to fulfill the requirements of each position. This is why you paused to consider requirements earlier- it is very easy to try to make things work when you're eager, desperate, or running on the rush of trying a new thing. Be patient: you don't want to be too hasty and accept a job that is not right for you or your skillset!

Instead, read the job posting once to get a sense of the overall specifications and tasks involved. Then read it again, carefully and slowly. If any word or words make you feel uncomfortable, bookmark that request so you can mull on it. You may feel pressured to respond to a posting, listing, or email from a prospective lead immediately, but it is far more important to respond honestly and accurately. If excitement had you skimming too quickly, you might miss out on very important details, like a due date that won't work for you, or a requirement that is outside your field of expertise.

Communication is, as they say, a two-way street. Depending on the type of side-hustle you choose, you may post ads, respond to postings, or reach out to various leads. Naturally, there is the chance that you may experience a few delays in communication. For example, someone might take several hours to receive your email, at which point you are occupied and cannot reply immediately. You might play phone tag for a few days. This is perfectly natural.

At this stage, many women share that they have encountered situations in which they were told that their response took too long, and as a result, the feedback indicated they were "unprofessional" or "unmotivated." While each of us may strive to provide fast and thorough responses, there are many responsibilities on our plates other than this side-hustle. You may wish to include a footer with your ad or email, explaining that you are only available after 7pm, Monday through Friday (as an example). Some women include a phrase in their profile or postings that they will not be able to respond to all inquiries immediately, as they have more urgent priorities. You won't be able to avoid people not reading this note, but you will have made every effort at transparency.

You may also wish to create your own website, blog, or social media site to advertise your services, as mentioned earlier. This is particularly helpful if you have many examples to share in your portfolio, or if you need a platform on which to advertise a larger variety of goods and services that you can provide. This is absolutely necessary if you want to conduct online marketing or influencer duties.

As you prepare to create an online space for your side-hustle, make sure you're confident in all of the content you post on your site, now and in the future. If you choose to blog or engage in social media, make sure you can update regularly- otherwise, your site will appear inactive and fall off of search engine inquiries and social media feeds.

A basic site should incorporate your profile, your portfolio, a full range of the different packages, products, or services you may offer as part of your side-hustle (as sketched out in the previous step), and a way for someone to contact you for more information. Make sure this contact information is accurate, and something that will neither be too annoying (such as your personal cell phone number) or too difficult to check (such as an email address to an account that doesn't load properly on your phone or device, or one that typically receives an overabundance of junk mail and spam). You may wish to create a brand new email account for your side-hustle. If you do so, don't forget to check it frequently!

Step 2: Interview Honestly

Honesty, clarity, and communication are three of the most important steps throughout the process of securing a side-hustle. During the interview process, these should be the guiding force behind every answer you provide to your potential client or customer.

You've shared with the whole wide world that you're available for your specific, self-tailored side-hustle. Over time, your ads, website, or postings have received some traction. As you experience a new influx of emails, online messages, phone calls, or orders, you will receive a barrage of questions: "Can you..." "Do you know how to..." "I'm looking for... " "Do you have... ."

These are normal questions, and though you might feel the answers are transparently displayed in numerous locations on your profile, portfolio, product page, social media, etc, do be sure to answer questions honestly. The four main rules of honest communication within your side-hustle interviews are:

1. *Do not oversell your availability.* You may have felt very confident earlier when establishing boundaries, but someone has just emailed you a very attractive offer, in which they're willing to pay $100 more if you can break your own rules about time and effort. They might petition for faster shipping, a tighter turnaround time, a larger project, extras, and other things which push your limits or are just outside of the boundaries you've set. It is ultimately your choice whether you wish to do that, but bear in mind: Your limits will be tested frequently. This is not the first time, nor will it be the last. Be consistent and straightforward, and even if you agree to the extras, make sure you note the exceptional situation.

2. *Do not undersell your skills.* You may be asked if you know about not only your competences, but adjacent talents. While it is typically not rude of someone to ask if something is in your personal toolbox, but you might feel as though you aren't qualified for what you do based on this extraneous request. The truth is that you are skilled in what you're doing, or you wouldn't be doing it! Even if your skills do not align with this individual's needs, they will be perfect for another situation.

3. *Always ask for a fair payment.* Many people will feel that, because this is a side-hustle for you, everything is negotiable. And in your business model, that might be true. However, it's important that you get equitable compensation for what you put into every gig. You might be tempted to float someone a freebie because "it was no big deal." But what happens when everyone requests freebies? Can your business model handle that?

4. *Establish reasonable turnaround times.* This refers to every contact you have with the people who provide payment in the realm of your side-hustle. From communications, to customizations, to scheduling appointments, to shipping timetables, make sure you are honest about what your client or customer can expect from you, and what actions or allowances you anticipate in return. An example of this is stating that you can provide edits.

Step 3: Get a Contract

Earlier, we talked about how some side-hustles require meeting specific quotas or requirements. Hand-in-hand with these quotas or requirements goes the definition of success.

Every single gig, even within the same field or with the same client, will have different requirements. In situations where you perform the exact same task repeatedly, there still might be variations. For example, a dog walker could walk three different dogs of the same breed the same distance on the same day, and one owner will be upset that the dog didn't receive enough exercise. You can submit three identical photos of three identical objects to three different photography clients, and none of them will like it. You can even send three bars of soap from the same batch to the same client, and they'll find that they didn't like the last one as much as the first one. There are critics everywhere, but their complaints or concerns don't mean that you failed at your task- only that you didn't communicate as well as you should have.

Consider the experience when you order a steak from a restaurant. The server will ask, "And how would you like that done?" Just as there's no one way to prepare a steak, there's no one way to get a job done.

Always ask your clients for the definition of success before you get started. For some contracting sites, such as those mentioned in the paragraph about requirements, it simply means meeting an established quota of purchases or reviews. As long as you're not incidentally upsetting their followers, customers, or shoppers, and making timely payments, you can carry on however you wish. Others might not care how you get to the solution, as long as you get the job done with the expected results. Still, others are performance-based in their judgment of your skills, so communication before you perform any tasks for them is absolutely key.

If you plan to clean houses, what tasks will your clients expect of you? Do they require a full antiseptic clean, or a brief sweeping and tidying up? If you're tutoring, do the students have to reach a certain grade within a specified time frame, or be prepared for a certain due date? If you're editing photos or documents, you've got to make sure you're not only prompt in delivery of a final project, but that the client likes what you've put together. The list goes on and on.

Therefore, it's very important to ask a client up front, "What does success look like to you?" For those who will perform direct services for a client, write down all the requirements for success or create a signed contract. This means that you won't stop working until you've met the terms of the contract, and they will pay you as long as you've performed all the tasks and delivered all the results requested in the contract. You need to take measures to ascertain your work is consistently judged, as well. If you are working for a pair of business partners, for example, and one loves your work, yet the other always complains, your best course of action is to take the time to communicate with each of them. A contract outlining your responsibilities can often save you (and your clients) loads of stress in this situation.

Some contracting sites, MLMs, or virtual employers will have contracts ready for you. Make sure you've read the "Terms and Conditions" carefully before signing. Ask questions as you need to, such as, "What happens if there's an emergency and I can't do x," or "Which of these is your highest priority?" This type of clarification is always appreciated, because it keeps communication honest and open.

Another important note about contracts: Once you have established one, do not start work until everyone has agreed or signed, as the process requires. This will save you a ton of heartache, stress, lost wages, and "he said/she said" arguments if anyone should disagree with any actions going forward.

Chapter 4: Establishing a Client Base

After some time, you will discover that you have established many contacts within your niche. For most side-hustles, the intention is to encourage a great many people to seek your goods or services, and having repeat customers or clients is often a very good thing. For example, creators will want people to consider them their primary source for wares in their niche. Resalers will want people to frequently browse their selections. Freelancers and online service providers also enjoy repeat business, especially if they have a great working relationship and have gotten to know each other well. In-person services also thrive from having a solid base of continuous customers, and those who work for MLMs will find that those who believe in your product will make up the most of their sales. Regardless of the gig you choose, impressing your customers and building your base is likely a goal.

The first rule of any business is that it is ok to start small. You may find yourself frustrated at how little your side-hustle has grown after a month. This is very normal. Don't let these feelings dissuade you from continuing on your path. Every small step is a step forward, so keep persevering.

There are ways to get the business you have to encourage growth. For example, you can ask people to review your business via your social media or website. If you do not have either of those, an option is to create a physical comment card or survey they can complete. You might even motivate them with a small discount or freebie. Your goal is to focus on the positive reviews, but even the not-so-positive write-ups will give you information about how your business is going.

Not-so-positive feedback can be difficult to accept, as some of us will feel taken aback or defensive when criticised harshly. You will also need to take some feedback with a grain of salt. There will always be circumstances out of your control, or a chain reaction of misunderstandings, or things that get lost or scrambled in transmission. Though the feedback from these instances might be harsh, your focus should be on YOUR actions throughout the process, and what you learned, overall.

At the same time, feedback is one of the most important things you can receive as your customer base expands, especially in the early stages of growth. So far, your side-hustle has existed only in your head. Now it's being put into play, and the best way to gain customers is to provide for them items and services they want, in a price range they appreciate, and exceed their expectations. Their reviews will tell you if you are succeeding or not, and help you find areas for improvement, and areas where you already excel.

You can share the positive feedback- with the permission of the person who wrote it- on your profiles, websites, or social media. Some freelance contracting sites, for example, offer a feedback and rating system within the app itself, which allows both the hiring party and the freelancer to share their thoughts and opinions about their part in the transaction.

Not only can you develop and grow your business from feedback, but from recommendations to others. If a person who enjoyed their experience with your side-hustle tells a friend, and that friend has a positive experience and tells THEIR friend, and so on... this is how you can very quickly build a following. You may wish to offer business cards with your contact information and website to clients, or set up a referral program so you can learn who has recommended your work to whom.

This is another provocative reason in favor of having an online presence through a website or social media, as these outlets can be very helpful for encouraging your side-hustle to grow. Word of mouth travels very quickly and can be often forgotten even faster. If someone recommends your work, the second person will likely search for your name or your business name. Make sure clients and customers can find you. All you need to share is enough information to confirm who you are and how to contact you!

The shelves of libraries and the pages of online searches are filled with the words of experts, who have written volumes intended to help others start a business and market their efforts both online and in person, so it would be impossible to capture all the different methods here. You may find, however, that after a certain period, things stop working as well as they used to. You might find an unexpected, unexplained lull in business. This might be normal and seasonal, depending on your particular gig, or it might be a sign that you need to re-examine your strategy.

Smart Boss Ladies strategize and re-strategize as necessary. Competition can be fierce no matter what niche you pursue. Think of the last time you saw a Grand Opening at a retail store or restaurant. At first, the parking lot was packed, and the lines were out the door! After some time, that levels off, and they hit a more regular pattern.

Once you feel like things have leveled off, think about what you can do to re-engage your side-hustle as needed. Maybe you're fine with a certain number of regular gigs. Perhaps you started this process with the intention of gaining a specific amount of extra income, and you've reached your goal. If life needs to renegotiate your time and availability, it's ok to back off of your gig for a bit. But if you want to keep things going, you've got to keep things fresh.

This is where it's great to have that network. People in your niche know how to keep your business thriving. People in your community know what inspires them to spend money. Thanks to the internet, you have hundreds of experts at your fingertips, so don't be afraid to reach out and explore options. Try new styles and alternative ways of doing things and see if they incorporate into your overall business plan. If not, simply dismiss that choice and move forward!

Take a Deep Breath Now and Then

You may go through a lot of talk before you take action, as the saying goes. You will very likely have waves, in which you receive a high volume of requests one day, then absolute silence for a bit. This is perfectly natural when it comes to hitting your stride in any new position or endeavor.

At first, you'll barely be able to contain your excitement at this new prospect, and maybe a bit apprehensive about how things will turn out. After all, this is a totally new experience. Even if you've worked in this field before, you're now working at your own discretion, in most cases. You might find yourself feeling very eager, or maybe experiencing new anxiety.

The whole purpose of doing that extra prep work is going to make sense now. You probably experienced some impatience with how slowly the first few steps seemed to drag, but this is why: once you launch your side-hustle, you'll find yourself awash with a bunch of emotions, and new demands will pull you into lots of different directions as things take off. By doing research, setting boundaries, and planning ahead before you even started marketing yourself, you saved yourself from having to make split-second decisions while your mind is already swimming.

SECTION 3:
KEEPING THE HUSTLE FRESH

At first, you'll have nothing but excitement for your brand new side-hustle. It's new to you, and you might be having fun with these first steps. Plus, the added income is always a bonus. There's a little apprehension about doing something new, and there will always be some frustrating moments that will leave you venting to a friend.

As time wears on, however, you might start feeling emotions that aren't quite so positive. You might start worrying that you made a bad decision, or that this is turning out horribly different from what you thought could happen. You might start dreading your side-hustle, cringing when you get emails, calls, or orders. Perhaps you have a streak of bad luck, frustrations, or disappointments. You might be tempted to drop your side gig and start again.

First, know that only you can make this decision. Make sure you give every potential option serious thought. Whether you choose to stop what you're doing immediately, or re-direct your side-hustle, you'll need to carefully consider each potential outcome. If you choose to try a different direction, try to go through all of the steps again. Some- like writing your profile- might comprise of just a few tweaks and edits. Other steps, such as planning your space and process, might require more tactical movements within your home and your life.

Before you scrap Plan A, however, know that this is a very typical, very normal part of any career path- side-hustle or no. Everyone finds a low point where they feel utterly discouraged. Everyone finds herself in a slump, with no active gigs, overly demanding requests, and no time. On top of that, everything in her personal life will become stressful, as well. Whether the stress of your side-hustle causes personal strife, or vice versa, is a philosophical argument you can consider later. In any case, you've probably heard that Murphy's Law dictates that everything will go overboard, all at once.

In this section, you'll get an understanding of not only the background efforts that will make day-to-day business easier for you, but also ways to support yourself mentally, emotionally, and physically so things continue operating at optimum capacity, even when that little voice in the back of your head encourages you to give up. It's ok- and very natural- to feel a little doom and gloom once in a while, but there's always an opportunity to pick back up and try again.

Chapter 1: Managing Money

The monetary side of things is often simultaneously the best and worst part about your side-hustle, so it only makes sense to tackle it first, head on!

For most of us women, the point of a side-hustle is to add some funds to our pockets and bank accounts. This might be for a specific reason, such as paying off student loans, buying a new car, or getting the kids ready for school. Alternately, you might just want to have a little extra feather in your nest, for future savings, retirement, and more. Regardless of what has inspired you to seek extra income, you will need to keep track of your income and expenditures. You'll want to keep thorough notes for all of your supplies, and the amount spent on everything. Then compare this to the various payments you received for each particular task for which you used those supplies. Take a look at a few examples to get a feel for the scope of this type of tracking:

Gig	Your Expenses	Your Payment
Resale: Refinishing antique furniture	Old chair: $40 Paint: $30 Paintbrushes: $15 Wood glue: $10 Clamps: $10 Ad posting: $2 Gas to drive the chair to new owner upstate: $30	Buyer Ms. Smith paid $200, PayPal, 1/12
Lawn service	Zero turn mower: $3000 Trailer for mower: $500 Weed wacker: $100 Rakes/tools: $20 x 5	Client Jones: $200 monthly, Venmopayment by the fifth Client Jackson: $100 weekly, cash each Friday Client Cortez: $50 per service, paid Venmo at time of service
Freelance Logo Design	Laptop for design: $2000 Design software: $200 External hard drive: $200 Graphics tablet: $1000 Physical sketch supplies: $50	Client A: $150, 11/11 via Venmo Client B: $500 for full package, 11/16 via Venmo Client C: Ongoing, $300 per benchmark, via Fiverr, $10 fee per benchmark
Candle Making	Wax: $10/unit Wicks: $10/unit Fragrance: $3/unit Molds: $5/unit Colors: $10/unit Equipment: $500 total Shipping materials: $50 total Shipping cost: $8 per candle	Order 1283: Paid $200 6/12 Order 1284: Paid $35 6/12 Order 1285: Cancelled Order 1286: Paid $42 6/18

These are only simplified examples, so your exact figures will vary, and will probably be much more comprehensive. You'll want to save receipts for each expenditure, whether those be digital copies, emailed order confirmations, or physical receipts from in-store purchases.

You'll want a dated record for each payment, as well. This might become a bit murky, especially if you're receiving payment through various means. You might receive cash payment for one task, then a Venmo payment for another, and payment through a contract site for yet another. You might receive funds on a specific schedule, or as services are rendered. If you work through another website or contract site, you might have to part with a portion of your payment as a fee or commission. This is why you looked very closely at the site requirements before you posted your profile.

But why all of this attention to detail? After all, this is just a casual side-hustle, right? Either you're making money or not!

In fact, there are many reasons to track every penny:

1. To make sure you're not spending more than you're earning
2. To help you track growth and trends, especially if you plan to make this gig last in the long run
3. For tax purposes
4. To ensure you're getting the payment you deserve

Now let's look at each of these reasons in more detail.

To make sure you're not spending more than you're earning
This is an incredibly important tenet on every level. First, by tracking the expenses that go into your side-hustle versus the payments you receive, you're able to determine if you're getting paid appropriately for the amount of effort you put into your side-hustle. By creating a chart similar to the one above, you'll be able to understand exactly where you have invested your money, and the overall return on investment.

This is true on the flip side, as well. Nearly everyone is excited about making more money, and the opportunities higher income can bring. It can be very tempting to spend your newfound income on something fun, like a night out with the girls, a new bath treatment, clothes, and more. It's good to "Treat Yoself" from time to time, but don't lose sight of what inspired you to engage in a side-hustle in the first place. Most of the gigs mentioned have frequent- if not constant- operating expenses. Your regular expenses aren't going to magically decrease, either. You'll still have the same bills you had before.

The best plan is to give yourself a monthly allowance, and tracking expenses and income related to your side-hustle in detail will help you better budget your allowance. As you can see from the examples above, everything is relative. A $500 payment for a project might seem really impressive until you consider that you still owe payments on the laptop you purchased to make this work possible.

At the end of the day, the decisions you make regarding your money are at your discretion. Your bills expenses your responsibility alone; however, it is never a bad idea to keep track of where your funds are going. Remember that you cannot always count on your side-hustle being a regular source of income; events in your personal life, your community, and even the world can impact the traffic you receive. You may encounter disputes about payments, have to provide returns or refunds, or take a loss if any of your investments go bad, break, or require service. Having a little cushion for your side-hustle can prevent you from struggling or making your overall personal financial situation worse.

To help you track growth and trends, especially if you plan to make this gig last in the long run

Every business experiences trends. Retail marketplaces experience a huge rush during the holiday season. Garden Centers turn into madness as spring approaches. During the summer months, travel is higher than any other time during the year, which impacts many industries. Even freelancers will note spikes in activity for particular niches like real estate or small business marketing, for example.

For every side-hustle you can consider, there will be seasonal high points and low points. Looking at a detailed recording of when you receive payments for which gigs will help you track these trends. Digging deeper into what each of those scenarios included will help you gauge when these high and low points occur, and what factors might motivate them.

Knowing when trends hit helps you perfect your timing, ramp up your marketing and advertising strategies, or prepare for the ups and downs of your business. You'll be able to proactively prepare, and take control of these changes from your side of the business.

One way to do this is by taking some chances in your business decisions once you have a feel for the overall trends. There is a process in marketing known as "A/B Testing." Nearly every business owner has tried this principle in some form at some point, though you might know it by a different name. The premise is simple: your current format is A, the control. B is something new. Something original. In marketing, a business owner might redesign their webpage, but only let certain people see the new page. Then they take account of the overall sales and reactions from page B to page A, the original page. Whichever version of the page performs best is the page the business owner releases to all viewers from then on (or until the next A/B testing phase).

As your own Boss Lady, you can consider doing this within the realms of your business. As mentioned earlier, you may have to strategize and re-strategize frequently, and recognizing the various trends in your business can help you stay on top of developments before they even happen.

For tax purposes

Tax requirements, regulations, and laws are different everywhere around the world, so it would be impossible to provide detailed advice on this topic.

That being said, the income you generate through your side-hustle may be taxable under your local, state, or federal guidelines. You don't want to find this out by surprise when your local tax authority sends you a nasty letter!

Ideally, you should research the tax implications of each individual gig you accept before you start working on it, but that's not always practical for each of us or for every situation. Your pet sitting client isn't going to wait patiently while you search for the different tax reporting regulations if they pay you via check versus cash. Instead, the most significant thing you can do is keep an extremely detailed record of all payments coming in and all expenses going out as it relates to your business.

You may also wish to consult with a tax professional in your area. There are plenty of resources online for most locations that can help you learn what earning limits and filing statuses have specific requirements, as well as what those requirements are. Links to a few of these resources are included at the end of this book, as well.

By tracking your purchases and income as each occurs, you won't find yourself scrambling to recall everything, scouring your inbox for receipts, or panicking come tax time. And in the worst-case scenario of dealing with a tax authority, you'll be able to clean matters up quickly, as long as you have easily accessed, easy-to-interpret records!

To ensure you're getting the payment you deserve
As noted earlier, it is highly likely that your business will take off very slowly. Even if you find yourself booked solid within minutes of posting your profile, you might feel most comfortable starting small with your offerings. Through the process of re-strategizing and growth, you may offer an increasing number of services, more time, and higher quality efforts to more people.

As your side-hustle grows and matures, make sure the payments you receive do, as well. If you feel the effort you provide has increased, or your skills have doubled, your pricing should reflect this. People do not expect to pay the same price for an amateur as they do for an expert, though those with existing relationships with your business may feel differently. You have the choice to offer special rates to those who have been with you from the beginning, but remember that your efforts should always be reimbursed adequately.

Chapter 2: The Birth of a Boss Lady

There's one thing that many people- both men and women- have a hard time saying. "NO." Especially in situations where saying "NO" can result in less pay, a lost client, or hurt feelings.

Even if you work in a position where you say "NO" regularly (or if you have small children!), turning down client requests may cause you to feel greater anxiety or apprehension in the context of your side-hustle. After all, the success of this business lies solely in your hands, and building a reputation of being hard to deal with isn't how you win business.

Still, it is very important that each of us work to maintain our professional integrity as Boss Ladies. Each step of this process has involved setting boundaries and enforcing those boundaries, while constantly evaluating room for growth and expansion, if possible. It is essential, as you develop professional relationships and an impeccable reputation in your field, that you continue to apply those boundaries equally to all customers, clients, and contacts.

Women in particular seem to be negatively typecast for being assertive. Without delving too deep into cultural or sociological theory, there are many reasons women are more reluctant to say "NO." You will need to say "NO" many times in the course of your side-hustle, but if you always communicate in a calm, rational, logical way, you will maintain your boundaries without becoming a bully or a victim. Further, remember that anyone who cannot conduct business with you in the same calm, rational, logical way is probably not someone you wish to do business with, anyway.

There are a few basic rules that will make saying "NO" much easier, while keeping customer, client, and contact satisfaction at an all-time high.

1. Do not take gigs you can't handle. Be reasonable with yourself. Make sure you have the time, the energy, and the supplies to do what is expected of you in the time frame requested. Remind yourself as often as necessary that though you wish to succeed in your side-hustle, there are other priorities in the forefront. Keep

yourself highly organized and be prepared to explain "unfortunately, I am not available."

2. Always be completely honest. Communication is one of the hardest things to master when running your own side-hustle. On one hand, you do not owe your clients, customers, or contacts any sort of detailed explanation about why you are saying "NO." However, there are plenty of people out there who cannot take "NO" for an answer. You might be familiar with the phrase "NO is a full sentence." This is true, especially for Boss Ladies. When challenged, your response can be very simple. "I do not have the capacity at this time" or "I am unable to fulfill that request right now. Thank you for your interest." If the other party cannot or will not respect that, it might be time to consider how valuable they are to the success of your business and find alternative options.

3. Do not sacrifice your well-being for a gig. Things are going to come up. There will be interference in your productivity. You might get delayed, waylaid, or even laid up for a period of time. If you need to sacrifice your side-hustle for any of these events, communicate this to your contacts. Again, you don't owe them an explanation unless you feel compelled to do so, but let them know your plans to step aside. If this is a temporary change, share with them when you expect to be back at it. If this is a permanent situation, thank them for their business and time. Some women thrive on all-nighters and tight deadlines, while others require a low-stress environment in which to fully focus. Never forget to honor your own needs and don't force yourself into commitments that can be damaging to your mental and physical health.

4. Do not let others pressure you into doing something you cannot do (time, cost, travel, etc). It can't be said enough: stick to your boundaries. There will be times when you'll be asked to do something that is on the border between what you can and cannot do. Carefully weigh your options here. Most people hate rejection, and some clients, customers, and contacts may try to negotiate and bargain with you to sway you to do something that might tiptoe what you can or will do in your business. Observe the boundaries you set, and when you make exceptions, make sure they are truly worth it. Also, if you find yourself in contact with another person who constantly uses overt pressure in attempts to persuade you otherwise, consider whether you need to be in contact with that individual.

5. Do not take less than you're worth. Anyone who has ever worked in a retail or restaurant job can tell you that customers will constantly try to haggle on prices, or declare that something "isn't worth the asking price." You have done the research, and you know that your rates and prices are fair. Therefore, you should always maintain your rates will not change just because someone feels they aren't right.

Be Assertive from Day 1

Early on, you may accept smaller, lower-paying gigs just to get the ball rolling. The metaphor usually compares these tasks to "low-hanging fruit." There's nothing wrong with pursuing these options- very frequently, doing a minor task now will lead to greater business and higher paying jobs in the future. Building your reputation and relationships with others in your business can be a process. However, there are many people who will try to take advantage of those who are new to a business in order to get a lot for a little. Even if

204

you want to build your portfolio with "incredible opportunities," make sure you are fairly compensated. Whether that means in payment, in rights, in barter, or some other manner, make sure you are not investing a lot of time and energy without somehow being reimbursed for your efforts. Learning is important, but not worth burning yourself out early.

Lastly, be careful about giving "freebies" and doing "favors," even for friends and family members. Again, it is at your discretion how you manage giveaways and discounts, but it can be very easy for people to take advantage of your kindness, even if they don't mean to. Be polite yet firm when someone oversteps your boundaries with their request, but don't give in if it compromises your integrity, even if the person doing the whining is a close relative.

A Note: To the Ladies Who Are Already Working Full-Time Jobs

As someone who has likely been in the workforce for a while, you probably feel like you've got this routine down pat. What the manager says is usually the final word on the matter. If you want to shake things up, then you better have a darn good reason. And for those who work directly with the public, the rules of customer service state that you are to always be polite, friendly and accommodating. The customer is always right, right?

That may be the case in your day job, but remember: YOU'RE the Boss Lady here.

It may surprise you to discover how quickly you slip into "day job" mode. You may find yourself trying to follow the policies and procedures of your current or recent full-time job. STOP THAT!

There will be policies that make sense in the realm of your side-hustle , and it's fine to adopt those. But if you wait to give yourself permission to innovate, strategize, or rework a certain place where things aren't working out quite right, you may work yourself into a roadblock. Stop waiting and do it now! There will be no board meetings, policy reviews, or complicated steps via HR. This is what being a Boss Lady is about- make your own decisions and run with them!

Chapter 3: Firing The Client

The phrase "Firing the Client" might sound serious and scary, especially if this is your first foray into running a business on your own. It sounds like a huge, dramatic hassle, and occasionally, it unfortunately pans out this way.

That being said, sometimes you need to stop interacting with someone from a business standpoint. Please note that the advice in this chapter not only goes for clients, but any contacts or services you might deal with in the course of your side-hustle.

There are many reasons you might need to do this:
- They are bullying you or harassing you
- They are defaming you, trying to use libel or slander to intimidate you or ruin your business
- They do not respond in a timely manner
- They do not pay as promised
- They have broken any part of the contract

This list is not all-inclusive, of course, and in many side-hustles, you'll have the option to communicate only with those who enhance and enrich your business. However, if you have a contract with a client or a third party service, you'll must review the "Terms and Conditions" you've agreed to before dismissing the unwanted contact.

Many third party services or hosting websites offer conflict resolution services, so be sure to check there first for assistance and guidelines. When communicating with these sites, you'll want to discuss your side of the issue openly and logically, without getting emotional. You may need to produce screen shots and copies of agreements. It may be tempting to give into the emotions you're having, such as anger, sadness, and frustration, but you must be calm and honest when dealing with conflict. Having a mediator can help mitigate these emotions, but they don't need to wade through your emotions, either. Keep notes of the issue at hand so you can be as efficient and patient when working through the issue with the third party.

If you work with the client directly, be sure to refer to any written agreements you have created with them during these conversations. Most viable contracts will have "escape clauses" that allow either party to walk away in the event of severe disagreement or turmoil. If this situation is not specifically mentioned in any type of binding agreement, then you need to be frank with your client. Tell them that this relationship is not working, and it is best for you to move on.

In many cases, this will be the end of it, but it is possible that clients who are behaving badly will escalate their behavior. Depending on your location, there may be online legal services available that will allow you to ask questions or clarify the steps you need to take in your country or state to legally stop the other party from harassing you or causing you harm. You may also need to speak with a small business lawyer, based on the situation at hand. In the "Resources" section, you'll find a few links that can help provide guidance if you discover you are stuck in a situation with a particularly awful connection.

This advice is also true if you need to sever ties with a supplier, a website, or someone who has been helping you on the business side. There's rarely such a thing as a conflict-free relationship with anyone, but in most cases, both parties are able to remain calm and communicate through the rough spots to reach resolution.

If you find yourself in constant combat with any of the people you regularly interact with through the course of your business, take the time to analyze whether they are providing you overall value. If you're constantly getting late orders, or there's always a mistake in fulfilling your requests, or your contact is just downright rude, take the time to shop around for someone else who can aid you in that capacity. While brushing off such behavior might seem tempting, since this is "just" a side-hustle, it's not fair to your mental health to constantly subject yourself to unnecessary high levels of stress. If you frequently lie awake at night, replaying conversations, or feeling general anxiety about having to deal with someone again, it might be time to consider other options.

There may be unfortunate occasions when that problematic individual is the only resource available to you. If this is the case, consider how you can relate your issues with them before they escalate into a scenario of harassment or other forms of bullying.

One popular method is to write a series of letters. The first letter you write allows you to express all the things you need to say, no holds barred. Do not send this letter. Tuck it away for a few days. Then write a second letter.

Draft this letter as if you might actually send it. Then tuck it away for a few days. The next step is to write out a third letter. This time, you can really type it into an email, but don't send it. Visit it a few times before you finally click send. The purpose of each letter is to help you better define why you feel the way you do, and what actions or behaviors you wish to discuss, without including too much frustration or emotion. Taking the time to reflect on each version of the letter will allow you the chance to process through the emotional content to find out what the actual problem is, allowing you to communicate more honestly and openly with more logic and reason than fear and anger.

A side-hustle is supposed to be a fun, easy, low-stress way of making money, so the hope is that you'll never encounter a situation such as this. If it does, remember to keep detailed records, follow the laws and stipulations of your contract. Above all, always stay calm!

Chapter 4: Don't Get Swept Away!

Having horrible interactions with customers, clients, and contacts is one side of the coin. The exact polar opposite of this situation is enjoying your side-hustle too much and letting it overtake your life.

For some women, this might not be a bad thing. Perhaps your side-hustle is something you've always wanted to do, but never thought you could do full-time. Once you become established, you might find that you can make a living this way, and dig into your new career with gusto.

For others, the rush you get from performing well on your side-hustle might find ways to interfere with your other scheduled activities. Unless you plan to turn this opportunity into a lifestyle, make sure you prioritize your needs and your life. Remember, this is a SIDE hustle!

Be sure to take time for you, or you'll quickly burn out on all of the requirements that are building up in your daily life. Self care is an extremely important part of a healthy mental, emotional, and physical lifestyle, so be sure you set aside time each day to take care of your own needs. Your wellbeing should be a huge priority for you!

While a few of us thrive on chaos, it may be essential for those women who are balancing school, family, or a full-time career with their side-hustle to set aside a specific time to work on projects and tasks related to your gig. As mentioned earlier, let your contacts know if there will be a delay in response time, but do not feel pressured to respond faster if it is not possible for your schedule. This goes hand-in-hand with establishing your boundaries and being empowered to say "NO." While everyone appreciates a quick reply to inquiries, most people understand that it's not always practical or possible to receive one. As long as you are meeting deadlines and providing clear communication within the expected timelines you have set with all of your contacts, you should not feel pressured to be more prompt.

Don't forget to take time to rest. Nearly everyone requires a little quiet time to themselves to recuperate. Make sure you're practicing healthy eating habits, sleeping as much as your body needs, and taking time to exercise throughout the week. Take part in activities that let you relax and calm your mind, such as coloring, reading, journaling, or taking a soothing bubble bath.

If you find yourself feeling weary or drained, you're likely not getting enough rest. If you are finding yourself feeling anxious or more emotional than usual, this can be another sign that you are more stressed than you realize. Another symptom that your work/life balance is off is feeling ill more frequently, or experiencing cold symptoms. When you feel something is off in your mind, body, or emotions, take the time to pause and reflect on your current schedule. Are you perhaps working too much? Have you extended yourself past your boundaries recently?

Though it may be difficult to stop the habits you have unconsciously developed in the process of your side-hustle taking off, it's very necessary to support a healthy work/life balance. You may tell yourself that you'll adapt to the new situation, and to an extent, that's true. However, every mind and body has its limits. If you find yourself making excuses to do something you normally wouldn't do, or you're experiencing mental or physical fatigue, it's time to stop and re-evaluate your plans and your actions.

Furthermore, do not compare yourself to others. There are many superstar women out there who seem to juggle absolutely everything a woman might want- a career, kids, media tours, websites and social media outlets, and they have rock solid bodies and perfect skin. If they can do it, then why can't you? Being inspired by these super-women is one thing. Sacrificing your well-being to emulate them is another. Don't allow yourself to become obsessed with anyone else's business. Your situation is strictly unique. Besides, everyone knows celebrities have personal assistants, nannies, tutors, managers, and web staff, as well as personal chefs, trainers, and make-up artists to help them with their success. You have only as much as you can reasonably give without sacrificing your higher priorities in life.

A Note: Organization Can Keep You On Track

One very important way to make sure your life doesn't become consumed by your gig is through impeccable organization. This is something that is hard for many of us, but can be the key to lowering your stress levels during busy days and weeks.

Many women enjoy using a planner or calendar to save all of their necessary tasks and deadlines in one place. Whether this is an app on your phone or tablet, a calendar reminder, or a physical planner that you carry with you through the day, decide on a method that will help you know what needs to be done and when. This will provide you the visual evidence you require of your plans and give you a chance to confirm and remind yourself of upcoming events. There are some apps, noted in the "Resources" section, that can import notifications from a variety of sources to make sure that nothing gets missed in the shuffle between texts, emails, orders, or syllabi.

You may also wish to create separate electronic folders for different types of correspondences. In some instances, you'll communicate with your contacts through a contracting site or website. Double check the guidelines for taking communications off of that site, as they may violate the "Terms and Conditions," or exempt you from future issue mitigation. Additionally, find out how long and under what circumstances you'll have access to that information.

Over time, you may discover that you need to screenshot important messages as reminders, or in case of future questions or concerns. Be sure to file those in an organized, uniform system you can easily access. Depending on the information in these screenshots, you might want to have these files password-secured, too. There are many business solution types of software and programs that can help with a variety of side-hustle record keeping needs. You can find a few examples listed in the "Resources" section.

Chapter 5: Continuing Education

One of the most exciting things about being human is that we never stop learning. Every day, we discover fresh information to inspire us.

Consider, for example, the popularity behind vision boards and sites like Pinterest, which allow us to collect pictures and links that capture our interest, and stimulate our thoughts and dreams. Our minds thrive on adding more knowledge and being asked to stretch just a little bit further.

Therefore, it's a great idea to put some of that self-improvement energy towards your side-hustle. Though there are businesses who proudly claim they've been doing things the same way for 50 years, that's not always feasible in an electronic, technology-driven world. Since the advent of the internet, it's become very evident that when a trend takes hold, it has everyone in its grips within seconds.

The heart of your business should consistently demonstrate your intentions, goals, and boundaries. Even though these elements may change over time, as you re-evaluate and re-strategize, you should never give up any of these three factors- this is why we worked so hard to brainstorm through these ideals early in the process.

That being said, growth is always possible. Whether that means growing in scope, in customer base, in products offered, or your own personal growth, some form of transformation is inevitable.

Doing the same thing day in and day out can get boring. As days and months go on and on, "boring" becomes "tedious." As years go by, "tedious" becomes mind-numbing. An under-stimulated brain becomes complacent. If you become too complacent, you just stop caring. And at that point, is it even worth it to continue?

Depending on your particular side-hustle, you might be ok with going into a fugue state and just getting things done. In other gigs, however, it can be a sign that the beginning of the end is nigh.

If your priorities and schedule allow it, consider devoting at least an hour a week to continuing education. The first thing that comes to mind is probably strenuous coursework. While that's certainly an option, if you choose to pursue it, the intention is less on adding degrees and certifications, and more on improving your techniques and tactics as an official Boss Lady.

There are many facets of the business world that you'll become increasingly familiar with as your business picks up, and it might become obvious at some point that you need to pause for a moment and focus on growth in one. This might include topics such as marketing yourself and building your brand, to using social media to streamline your business. You might wish to learn more about developing your own website, including a foray into HTML coding... or maybe learning more about organizational opportunities is more your style.

All women can benefit from an occasional refresher course on how to effectively run a business. Whether the material covered is brand new or familiar territory, it never hurts to have a reminder of what we're doing successfully, and areas where we might require improvement. When we work for others, we have the benefit of frequent feedback and performance reviews to keep us focused on goals and objectives. When acting as our own Boss Lady, we might figure that everything is fine as long as nothing's broken, so to speak.

Try to seek out resources that will encourage you to continue performing effectively. This might be an interactive talk given at your local library or coffee shop, or an online forum for women who are running their own side-hustle from home. You might take part in short seminars that focus on growth and development from a business perspective, or take part in courses that offer tips and tricks for specific elements, including communication, organization, and more. Try a few different options to see what resonates most with your creativity and learning style.

One area in which we might need regular inspiration is in marketing yourself and your side-hustle. The trends in marketing change very rapidly, so if you plan to spread the word about your gig, maintain that excitement over time, you'll want to keep your eye on those trends. This can include frequently revisiting your profile and portfolio, evaluating the user experience of your website, taking new pictures of your products to share on your selling walls, and revamping descriptions to be more exciting.

If a blog is not already an integral part of your side-hustle, you might weigh the options of starting one, as it can bring attention to your side-hustle through organic traffic. That means that anyone searching your niche might stumble upon your blog and find your journey interesting. This may lead them to learning more about you through your social media, and contacting you about the opportunities through your hustle. If you do this, perhaps blogging is an area in which you'd like to extend your knowledge, with online courses or via writing forums for business women.

Your niche is another area in which you can continue your education. While you're obviously very good at what you do, there are probably areas in which you can improve, if you're being honest with yourself. If you feel like every client or project is blurring together after a period of time, it might be wise to diversify your portfolio a bit within your niche.

First, consider exploring trends in your area of expertise. If you type the words that describe your side-hustle into a search engine, what are some of the results? If you scroll to the very bottom of the page, what are some related searches? What ideas do these give you about your own business?

Consider also the feedback you receive. If someone says "I was expecting X, but I got Y," try to learn more about the first option. Is this something you can offer? What would it take to learn X? Would it be worth the investment?

Next, think of your own dreams. Once you've repeated the process of your particular side-hustle a few times, you might start having thoughts such as "It would be really neat if I could..." or "I wonder if I could find a way to... ." These reflections are a sign that your brain- and your business- might be eager for the next level. Take some time to follow that train of thought. What time, money, supplies, etc would you need to take that step? Would your contacts be interested in the results?

From there, let your mind wander. What are some skills that might not be directly in your niche, but can compliment your current side-hustle? For many gigs, you may identify ways to creatively enhance your offerings and availability. For example, if you're a pet sitter, perhaps you learn how to perform basic grooming techniques, beyond wash and dry. If you are watching children as part of your gig, maybe you introduce tutoring capabilities. If you're in the resale business, what are some restoration methods that could amplify your ability to refurbish and repurpose the items you find?

For every business there's a way to go just a step further. Maybe you're not ready to take a secondary plunge today, but as you get settled in with your new endeavor, some ideas might take seed and start to sprout. Don't automatically dismiss them, just because the timing isn't right; instead, jot them down somewhere you won't forget them. Revisit them often. Talk to others about your ideas.

Every level of your side-hustle has a "next level." Business women in all corners of the world are constantly revisiting their processes and innovating. In the beginning of this chapter, we discussed how "continuing education" might bring to mind coursework and formal classroom environment. If that's something that can sharpen your business skills, why not check out your options? As pointed out, some side-hustles require licensing or certification- find out what steps are involved in that, they expand upon it. If you're doing well with affiliate marketing, why not dive deeper into the world of marketing by taking a few online courses? Obviously, you need to be cognizant of the time, money, and effort you have available for these things, but investments in yourself can pay out huge dividends over time.

Last, the phrase "continuing education" should likewise apply to your own wellness. Your side-hustle should help you learn and grow as a person, within your own life. Rather than simply sucking your resources dry for the sake of money, the goal is that your work will help you learn about yourself. You'll quickly understand a lot more about your organizational style, your communication approach, and things that trigger both positive and not-so-positive emotions. Don't tune yourself out through this process. Instead, take the advice in this book and approach it from your own, individual, unique place. You will make mistakes, and things will happen that you won't necessarily enjoy, but always attack opportunity with honesty, patience, and grace, and watch those qualities spill out into your "real" life.

FINAL THOUGHTS FOR
THE BOSS LADY-TO-BE

The preceding pages have provided thoughts, insights, guidance, and recommendations based on the very real experience of finding, acquiring, and maintaining a side-hustle.

A side-hustle is, in many senses, like having a full-time job. You must exercise discipline. Maintaining organization is an absolute necessity in all facets of your life now. You need to monitor your efforts and expenses to make sure the output matches the input. Customer satisfaction is also highly important.

In other ways, it's unlike anything you've ever undertaken. A side-hustle is incredibly unpredictable. The rules are what you say they are. You have independent control over what you get done, and when you do it. Instead of managers and supervisors measuring your productivity and success, YOU are in charge of your fate. You are the judge of whether you did a great job, or whether it's an opportunity to do better next time.

Unpredictability is one thing that might have prevented you from finding a side-hustle in the past. The "feast or famine" adage is very commonly thrown around by those who work a variety of gigs. There will be times when you'll be incredibly busy. There will also be times when you are so focused on other things, you might forget that you actually had a side-hustle to begin with. If the idea of regular, identical paychecks makes you feel most comfortable, you might have trouble adapting to the side-hustle life.

The emotional side effects of a side-hustle is also something that will be new. You _will_ be frustrated. You _will_ receive discouraging comments. You _will_ be upset, and you will likely make someone else feel upset, whether you mean to or not. Side-hustles are a bit of a "lawless" territory, and all the societal norms you might recognize from corporate, full-time job settings might go out the window immediately in times of conflict. But unlike at a full-time job, you don't have coworkers to take you out to happy hours and sympathise with you. You can't go to HR and file a complaint. You have to deal with every situation head on, and it can be very uncomfortable territory, especially at first.

But more importantly, your side-hustle may be an amazing opportunity for you to express yourself and your creativity while getting paid. Many people feel that diving into their side-hustle is one of the most rewarding experiences of their professional life. You get to make your own policies and procedures. As the Boss Lady, you only invest what you want to invest, and you make the money you need. In fact, you can earn money while you're asleep, in your pajamas, driving your kids to school, or in between research papers.

Most of all, side-hustles give us the opportunity to celebrate something we truly enjoy. There are many, many women who have made their side-hustle a full-time job, simply because they love what they do. It's impossible to say whether you'll make the same amount of money, more, or less if you go after your gig... that all depends upon your niche, and your own personal effort into developing your brand and your business. However, there might be an opportunity for you to take things to the next step, and the next step, and so on, until that little hobby that you turned into a brief gig has become your whole empire. Don't dismiss it!

On the other hand, your side-hustle may be short lived. You might find interest is little, with few communications inquiring about your availability. That doesn't mean you're doing anything wrong. It shows that this is not the right time for that particular gig. As mentioned before, re-strategizing is the best way to get past this. Sometimes the slightest adjustment in your business strategy will set you on the path to success.

If you intended for your side-hustle to serve only as a temporary fix to a financial situation, don't be surprised if you find that you miss the work, once you've wrapped up those final tasks and ended things. You might miss the connections you had, or performing certain functions. That's a sure-fire sign that your gig was the ideal one for you. And who's to say? Once things settle down a bit, maybe you find a way to integrate the skills you used in your little business in your full-time life?

As you get started, remember there are many resources out there to help guide you. A small handful of those are included in the "Resources" section. While you might typically skip that type of information, you might need an extra leg up in finding exactly the niche you wish to occupy, and what options, opportunities, and requirements might lie ahead of you as you approach this new phase in your life.

Finally, as you set down this book and start brainstorming, keep in mind the tenets of honesty, integrity, and communication, as mentioned frequently throughout the preceding chapters. The challenges and rewards of your side-hustle will be many, but as a Boss Lady, you are always in control of how YOU act, how YOU communicate, and how YOU react. Make sure that you always do so with the best intentions, and with full clarity. At the end of the day, you can only do your very best, and if you feel satisfied that you have, then you have truly succeeded.

Best wishes for the brightest future!

SECTION 4:
RESOURCES

It's hard to get started if you don't know where to start. Even Dorothy wasn't sure where to go until she was shown the famous Yellow Brick Road! To get you started on your path to Boss Lady stardom, here are a few links.

None of these links are intended to be considered endorsements, and may not reflect the opinions of those affiliated with this book. These are simply a few popular resources from around the internet that can provide you with useful information and get your own search headed in the right direction. We cannot vouch for the success you might find through these resources, and encourage you to use them as a launch pad for the detailed research any woman needs to do when preparing for her brand new side-hustle. Remember... you are empowered as a Boss Lady, and your success is all within reach!

Resources to Get You Started In The Right Direction

These resources should get you thinking about the type of side-hustle you might like to take on and inspire you to jot down a few ideas of your own. We've spotlighted a few industries here, choosing sites that provide the greatest variety of options. Again, we can't guarantee your success, but perhaps, if you check out a few of these options, you'll find an ad, blog post, or even a small paragraph that sets your creativity in motion!

Freelancing Networking Sites

To help you get started, here are a few popular sites for finding freelance work. The current categories of work are included for each, but note, there are literally hundreds of subcategories involved. You can connect with folks around the world who are looking to fill all sorts of positions, from hiring their own personal astrologer to finding someone who can photograph their jewelry!

Upwork: www.upwork.com

Types of jobs: Web, Mobile & Software Development, IT & Network Support, Data Science & Analytics, Engineering & Architecture, Design and Creative, Writing, Translation, Legal, Administrative Assistance, Customer Service, Sales, Marketing, Accounting

Fiverr: www.fiverr.com

Categories: Graphics & Design, Digital Marketing, Writing & Translation, Video & Animation, Music & Audio, Programming & Tech, Business (includes consulting, planning, marketing, and branding, plus others), Lifestyle (includes online lessons, arts, coaching and much more), Industries (includes Gaming, Architecture, Real Estate, Political Campaigns, etc)

People Per Hour: https://www.peopleperhour.com/

Service types: Technology & Programming, Writing & Translation, Design, Digital Marketing, Video & Photo & Image, Business, Music & Audio, Marketing, Branding & Sales, Social Media

Freelancer: https://www.freelancer.com/

Categories Include: PHP, Website Design, Graphic Design, Mobile Apps, Android Apps, iPhone Apps, Photoshop, Logo Design, Article Writing, Data Entry, Internet Marketing, SEO, 3D Modelling, Copywriting, Ghostwriting, Linux, Amazon Web Services, Banner Design, Software Development, Accounting, Finance, Legal, Manufacturing, Logistics

In- Person Hustles:

When you were younger, you might have written flyers, or knocked on your neighbours' doors to let them know that you were eager to help with odd jobs, babysitting, pet sitting, and more. Today, the internet allows us the ability to connect with nearly everyone in your area. The following sites are offered to those who wish to post their services publicly, so that those who are looking for their skills can find them easily. It's much more efficient than going door-to-door!

105 Ideas for your Service Businesses: https://www.entrepreneur.com/article/80684

As you do your research, you'll find loads of articles on this topic. This article in particular from Entrepreneur.com goes further down the rabbit hole of potential in-person hustles than we could, with over 100 ideas for starting up a small service business in your area! Included in this article are resources for further reading, as well.

TaskRabbit: https://www.taskrabbit.com/

Tasks Include: Handyman Services, Hauling Services, Help Moving, Hire a Personal Assistant, Minor Home Repair, Hire a Painter, Yard Cleanup & Removal, Delivery Services, Laundry Services, IKEA Furniture Assembly, TV Mounting, Hanging Pictures Help, Furniture Delivery, Light Installation, Closet Organizing Services, Furniture Removal, Furniture Movers, Disassemble Furniture

If you'd like to interact with animals more for your side-hustle, check out these sites, where those who provide pet-related services- from walking, to sitting, to grooming, and more- can connect with potential clients:

www.Rover.com

www.Petsitter.com

www.Sittercity.com

www.dogvacay.com

Home care for seniors, adults, and children is also a very valuable business that might be a great option for you. Below, we've included a few sites that can connect you with those looking for a helping hand with their family members:

https://www.care.com/

https://www.urbansitter.com/

https://www.sittercity.com/

https://www.seekingsitters.com/

Tutoring is another great way to help others and provide your services and knowledge through your side-hustle. Here are some sites that could connect you with people who can benefit from your skills.

https://tutors.com/pro

www.care.com

https://heytutor.com/tutoring-jobs/

https://tutorextra.com/

Affiliate Marketing Information

Affiliate Marketing is a bit of a new field that has developed quickly as many businesses take to the internet to share their products with the world. Here are a few sites that explain the process in more detail, provide education, and connect future affiliate marketers with gigs.

Lists of potential Affiliate Leads:

A List of Affiliate Programs from Authority Hacker

"101 Best" from Millennial Money

Additionally, the site ClickBank is a stepping stone for many who are new to the idea of affiliate marketing. www.clickbank.com

Time Management Help

As women with what feels like a million priorities on our plates, we could all use a little help with time management. Too often, you might find yourself saying, "I'll start on that once I finish this," but before you know it, it's midnight, and there's no more extra time!

These apps and programs may help you identify your commitments and stay on task all day. Since there are so many different versions of time management tools, we've included a few different options. Some help you track time to create better habits, others offer full service assistance to keep you moving forward, even when challenges stack up.

My Life Organized: https://www.mylifeorganized.net/
Available for: iOS and Android, Windows
What it does: If your "To Do" list has its own "To Do" list, you might be the type to appreciate My Life Organized. This app breaks down all of your duties into tasks, all of your tasks into sub-tasks, and all of your lists into errands.

RescueTime: https://www.rescuetime.com/
Available for: iOS and Android
What it does: This app works in the background, keeping track of your internet behavior. If you're the type who easily falls down internet rabbit holes, this is a way to keep you focused on your new goals, rather than getting distracted. For those getting started with a side-hustle for the first time, apps like this might help you gain accountability, and lessen stress.

Timely: https://memory.ai/timely

Available for: iOS and Android, Mac and Windows

What it does: Timely learns about your behaviors and tasks and creates schedules to help optimize your time. If you need help with accountability and staying on track with multiple projects, this type of AI app can be of assistance.

Toggl: https://toggl.com/

Available for: iOS, Mac, Android

What it does: Toggl is a time-tracking app that helps you see where you're spending the most of your time. Reports provide weekly, monthly, or annual reports to help you refocus on your time and efforts.

Trello: https://trello.com/

Available for: iOS and Android, Mac and Windows

What it does: Trello is a visuals-based project management program. It's fully customizable, so as your side-hustle takes off, you can create various project boards to track absolutely everything.

Website Building Tools for Business Owners

If you're building a website as part of your side-hustle, you'll want to make sure you do it right. Whether you're an old pro at web dev, or you're not entirely sure what you're doing, the internet is full of resources that can help simplify the process. In the end you'll have a basic, professional-grade website that provides your potential customers with all the information they need about you and your side-hustle.

Again, these are not designed to be considered endorsements or affiliations.

The following are just a handful of the popular website building tools for small businesses. Always double check the costs, the ease of use, the features, and limitations for each option before you proceed!

Go Daddy: www.godaddy.com

Go Daddy has a strong reputation for being easy to use for basic websites. It doesn't offer tons of customized options, but you can select from a few different packages to create the online presence you're looking for.

Squarespace: www.squarespace.com

Squarespace is another website builder that offers simplicity and custom options. The package options can be selected to support your basic profile and portfolio, or can include an online store and blog.

Wix: www.wix.com

Wix is designed for true online businesses, rather than simple web pages, so while it can be more expensive than some competitors, it's because it is designed to include all of your ecommerce needs, with higher storage rates and bandwidth for more traffic. Wix is well-known for its ease of use and it's high customization capabilities, which makes it ideal for those whose side-hustle might someday become a full-time gig.

WordPress: www.wordpress.com

WordPress is very popular for building online businesses, but it's not the simplest site to maneuver. There are seemingly endless widgets and plug-ins that can be added to a WordPress site, which are mostly meaningful for Boss Ladies who are looking to create a full online business, rather than a simple "About" page.

Marketing Guides for Small Business Owners

As internet marketing has taken off, so has the business of internet marketing gurus. There is valuable information to be found in nearly every corner of the internet.

If you have a limited perspective on how to market yourself and your business, you may wish to look into some educational options offered via the internet. Some of these offerings come free of charge; others are offered at a nominal fee.

Additionally, some of these are going to be more valuable to you than others. In every case, check out the course description, and learn as much as possible from reviews and any samples that are offered. The following list includes courses that are either taught or written by women, or are woman-positive in their approach. This list is in no way all-inclusive, but a place to start for easy education options at home.

LinkedIn Options

Academy.Business

SCORE

Udemy Basics

U.S. Small Business Administration

Taxes and Money Management

The great part of a side-hustle is bringing in that sweet, well-earned pay. However, your new source of income may change the way you or your family file taxes. The following resources, including articles, websites, and financial review specialists for women, may help you understand the tax implications of your new gig. Due to the publishing location of this book, these sites are largely based in the United States. If you are managing your side-hustle from another part of the world, you may wish to check with your local tax authority for more details.

You may also wish to consult with a local CPA or financial advisor for details on how your taxes might be handled at a local level.

A Freelancer's Guide to Taxes, From Turbo Tax: https://turbotax.intuit.com/tax-tips/self-employment-taxes/a-freelancers-guide-to-taxes/L6ACN-fKVW

Small Business and Self-Employed Business Center: https://www.irs.gov/businesses/small-businesses-self-employed

Tax Tips for Side Jobs: https://turbotax.intuit.com/tax-tips/self-employment-taxes/side-giggers-tax-tips-for-side-jobs/L6025l8Uh

Tax Information for Freelancers, Artists, Writers, and Psychotherapists: https://www.freelancetaxation.com/

Tax Consequences of a Side Hustle: https://money.usnews.com/money/personal-finance/taxes/articles/2018-03-01/the-tax-consequences-of-your-side-hustle

Women's Wealth Connection: https://waasset.com/services/womens-wealth/

Legal Support

From helping with review of contracts, to mitigating potential lawsuits, having legal support might be helpful for your particular side-hustle. A small business lawyer can also make sure you've got all the t's crossed and i's dotted when it comes to the licensing and insurance requirements of your new side-hustle.

Yes, legal fees are expensive, but not nearly as damaging as court fees, IRS notices, and paying out damages due to something you didn't know was your liability. The following links lead to online legal support systems that can help you get all the details sorted... or help you out when things get messy.

LegalMatch: https://www.legalmatch.com/
If you're not sure who to call, or where to get started, LegalMatch allows you to answer questions to help pair you with local expertise.

Rocket Lawyer: https://www.rocketlawyer.com/
This site covers most major legal events, but specifically includes a start up business section, and a section for creating easy-to-use legal documents.

SCORE: https://www.score.org/legal-issues-resources
SCORE is an all-around fantastic resource for small business owners, and while some of their information is less geared towards the side-hustle and more towards full-time businesses, there's plenty of helpful information on their site for any woman who works on a smaller scale.

US Department of Justice: https://www.justice.gov/eoir/list-pro-bono-legal-service-providers
Click by state to find those in your area who can provide legal services or advice at no cost to you.

Support Groups/Forums/Blogs

As a woman starting out with her first side-hustle, you may feel like you are treading water in uncharted territory. The good news is that there are many sites out there that provide women with encouragement, resources, and networking opportunities for every facet of Boss Lady life.

Each of these sites provides helpful resources for women who are trying to balance life with a side-hustle. Whether that's networking opportunities, articles, webcasts, podcasts, blogs, or educational tools, each of these sites could enrich your experience as a woman with a successful side-hustle, and to open opportunities for future growth, streamlining the process, and more.

Again, this is not intended to be an endorsement of any of these organizations; however, we recognize that these are some of the most popular resources for women in every aspect of the workforce. As your personal network grows, hopefully you'll continue to connect with others who can provide you with support and advice for your side-hustle, life's daily challenges, and beyond. We all need a helper sometimes!

American Business Women's Association (ABWA): https://www.abwa.org/ From the site: *"The mission of the American Business Women's Association is to bring together business women of diverse occupations and to provide opportunities for them to help themselves and others grow personally and professionally through leadership, education, networking support and national recognition."*

The BOSS Network: http://www.thebossnetwork.org/

About the "Bringing Out Successful Sisters" Network: *"Our mission is to promote and encourage the small business spirit and professional development of multicultural women. The BOSS Network is a community of career and entrepreneurial women who support each other through conversation, online and event-based networking."*

Ellevate Network: https://www.ellevatenetwork.com/
For women who wish to rise and thrive in their chosen profession. *"We believe that when ambitious professional women get more opportunity it ultimately benefits everyone, and leads to a more equal world. We're committed to giving these ambitious professional women the community they need to take the next step in their careers — whatever that means to each of them."*

eWomen Network, Inc.: https://www.ewomennetwork.com/
Touted as "The Premier Success System for Women Entrepreneurs," their mission is *"to help women launch, grow and scale your business. We are a network of over 500,000 women connected through 118 chapters across the United States, Canada, Australia and the United Kingdom."*

FreelanceMom: http://www.freelancemom.com/
Created by a real mom who chose the entrepreneurial route, Lisa Stein's site intends to *"merge women and information together to transfer knowledge, inspiration, wisdom and actionable solutions so you can find the work you love through entrepreneurship."*

Mompreneur Center: https://www.entrepreneur.com/topic/mompreneurs
This special area of the famed Entrepreneur.com e-magazine is dedicated to real moms and women who balance their hustle with the demands of full-time parenting. Articles of encouragement and advice cover a variety of topics, from the practical to the emotional.
Project: She Went For Her Dreams: http://www.shewentforherdreams.com/

Ariane Hunter's Project #SheWentForHerDreams *"started as a roundtable conversation with her sisterhood about life, work, and the pursuit of passions has turned into a rapidly growing collective of women who have joined the movement of dreamers and doers everywhere."*

Side Hustle Nation: https://www.facebook.com/groups/sidehustlenation/
The Facebook forum to compliment SideHustleNation.com and The Side Hustle Show podcast. This is a place to interact with others at all stages of their side-hustle, for inspiration, guidance, and support.

TED for Women: https://www.ted.com/topics/women+in+business
The site is a centralized collection of TED talks provided for and by women in business. Choose from a variety of fields and playlists to watch the talk you need to motivate you at any stage in your side-hustle.

The Penny Hoarder: https://www.thepennyhoarder.com/
This site includes a large variety of information regarding making money, saving money, and what to do with the money you have. *"Founded in 2010, The Penny Hoarder is one of the nation's largest personal finance websites. Its purpose is to help people take control of their personal finances and make smart money decisions by sharing actionable articles and resources on how to earn, save and manage money."*

Women Entrepreneur: https://www.entrepreneur.com/women
Another section of Entrepreneur.com, Women Entrepreneur provides a bevvy of resources for women embarking on their first side-hustle, including courses, expert mentors, and plenty of insight to help ladies through the process of launching a successful hustle.

Women in Technology International: https://witi.com/

Started in 1989 as The International Network of Women in Technology became one of the premier trade associations for women in technological fields. Today, WITI's three million professionals, 60 networks and 300 partners worldwide work to: *"Empower innovators.*

Inspire future generations. Build inclusive cultures."

Women's Venture Fund: https://womensventurefund.org/

"Founded in 1994, The Women's Venture Fund (WVF) is a nonprofit organization that helps women to establish thriving businesses in urban communities with funding and business development programs." Their site is also full of resources and stories to help women new to the world of business find their way.

Working Moms Connection: https://workingmomsconnection.org/

WMC is an American non-profit organization that helps mothers juggle the needs in both their professional and personal lives, in order to give each woman the help they need to find success in both. This includes educational opportunities, peer coaching, and business coaching. WMC values Courage, Self-Worth, Diversity, and Transparency amongst its members.

Reviews

Reviews and feedback help improve this book and the author. If you enjoy this book, we would greatly appreciate it if you could take a few moments to share your opinion and post a review on Amazon.

Printed in Poland
by Amazon Fulfillment
Poland Sp. z o.o., Wrocław

67136837R00137